# FRONT COVER

INSIDE FRONT COVER

# STUDY GUIDE FOR THE PMI RISK MANAGEMENT PROFESSIONAL® EXAM

*Second Edition*

**Abdulla J. Al Kuwaiti,**
RMP, PMP

Printed in the United Arab Emirates

**Copyrights (c) 2013 by Abdulla J. Alkuwaiti**

All rights reserved. No part of the contents of this book may be reproduced or transmitted in any form or by any means without the written permission of the author

Examples and exercises in this book are fictitious. No association with any real company, product, name or event is intended or should be inferred

This book expresses the author's views and opinions. The information contained in this book is provided without any express, statutory, or implied warranties. The author will not be held liable for any damages caused or alleged to be caused, either directly or indirectly, by this book

"PMP," "RMP," "PMBOK," and "PMI" are marks of the Project Management Institute, Inc. All trademarks are trademarks of their respective owners

# Table of Contents

## Chapter 1:
| | |
|---|---|
| Introduction | 02 |
| The "Memorize then Understand" Framework | 04 |
| First, Know the Rules of the Exam | 04 |
| More on the PMBOK | 05 |
| How to Apply for the RMP Exam | 07 |

## Chapter 2:
| | |
|---|---|
| Essentials | 12 |
| What You Need to Know to Prepare for the Exam | 12 |
| The Risk Model | 12 |
| Expected Monetary Value (EMV) | 16 |
| Three-point Estimation | 16 |
| Decision Trees | 17 |
| Earned Value Analysis (EV) | 20 |
| Modeling and Simulation | 21 |
| Probability Distribution | 26 |
| Sensitivity Analysis | 28 |
| Contract Types | 29 |
| Assumptions | 30 |
| Work Breakdown Structure (WBS) | 32 |
| Quality Tools | 33 |
| Leadership Styles | 35 |
| Motivation Theories | 37 |
| Organizational Structure | 38 |

## Chapter 3:
| | |
|---|---|
| Communication and Stakeholders | 44 |
| Stakeholders | 44 |
| Communication Basics | 46 |
| Communication Methods | 48 |
| Communication Technology | 49 |
| Communication Skills | 50 |
| Stakeholder Identification (The Stakeholder Register) | 51 |
| Stakeholder Classification | 51 |

## Chapter 4:
| | |
|---|---|
| Introduction to Risk Management | 56 |
| The Risk Management Processes | 57 |
| When to Start Risk Management | 59 |

## Chapter 5:
Inputs/Outputs 64
Tools for Risk Planning 64
Tools for Risk Identification 66
Tools for Qualitative Risk Assessment 70
Tools for Quantitative Risk Analysis 72
Tools for Risk Response 74
Tools for Risk Monitoring and Control 81
Inputs for Risk Management 82
Outputs 86
Inputs and Outputs 87
Risk Management Plan 88
Project Management Plan 90
Risk Register 91

## Chapter 6:
Exercises to Remember Inputs Outputs and Tools 98

## Chapter 7:
Risk Management Processes 120
Process One: Risk Planning 121
Process two: Risk Identification 125
Process three: Qualitative Risk Analysis 131
Process four: Quantitative Risk Analysis 134
Process five: Risk Response Planning 138
Some Terminology 143
Process six: Risk Monitoring and Control 146

## Chapter 8:
Practice Questions 156
Question Types 157
Questions on Where to Find Information 157
Before You Start with the Questions 160
Questions 161
Answers 187

## Chapter 9:
Can you do it? 208
Additional concepts 209
Recap 214

After you Pass? 220
References 221
Index 222

To my mother, my wife and the "brilliant four"

# A Word on Professional Certification

There is a lack of undergraduate courses in risk management. Fortunately, the lack of undergraduate courses is compensated by the availability of professional certification.

I am pro-professional certification in any area. Its not only the exam that distinguishes you, but your efforts to register and study, especially as a working professional. This gives positive indications about a person's commitment and professionalism.

Acquiring the Risk Management Professional® credentials will make your level of expertise and knowledge of the subject recognized. Passing the exam requires quite an effort from you and that effort will definitely reflect on your work.

Having a certificate in your pocket shouldn't be your ultimate goal; rather, it is a means to support your pursuit of excellence and professionalism. Don't stop at the RMP exam, there are many other standards and it will be a good idea to explore them. Being certified has had a positive impact on me and it made me part of a community that encourages knowledge sharing on the subject of "risk".

# About the Author

Abdulla Al-Kuwaiti finished his BSc in Systems Engineering in the University of Arizona, in 2000. Shortly after, he joined a major oil company as a Safety Engineer. Since then, he has been introduced to risk management, trained on it and is practicing it on a daily basis.

He achieved his Masters in Project Management in 2007 and now works as a Program Manager. Abdulla is RMP and PMP certified by the Project Management Institute in the USA.

You may contact the author at:
alk.books@gmail.com
www.kuwaitat.net

*Other books by Abdulla :*

In Arabic, English & German

# Chapter 1:
## Introduction

# Introduction

Well done, you want to be a Risk Management Professional (RMP). Let me congratulate you on this decision for two reasons: first, you believe that Risk Management is important and worth your time and money; second, you are choosing a well-known and reputable certification body: the Project Management Institute (PMI®).

**Why I Have Written This Book**

I have been involved in risk management since the year 2000. My appreciation for its simplicity and effectiveness has continued to grow and flourish more and more. Risk management is a management concept that is easy to implement, has a positive effect on different areas and applying it can lead to remarkable improvements at work.

If you think about it, planning for a project depends on assumptions and estimations, which can be right or wrong. We plan in a linear and logical way, but our world seldom goes in the same way. Things are not better during project execution where changes and new events can distract a project manager from seeing the whole picture. Risk management comes to play here as an eye-opener and a "Pull-Every-Thing-Together Mechanism" to help the project manager and his/her team, along with the stakeholders, make sense of how different elements come together in a project.

---

**Risk Management as a "pull everything together"**

If I had to choose one knowledge area to focus on in my project, it will be risk management. As you will see in the book, risk management will question and test your time and money estimations, communication plans, contractual agreements and quality requirements. By implementing risk management, you will be able to identify mistakes and misalignments, and increase the probability of project success.

---

# Introduction

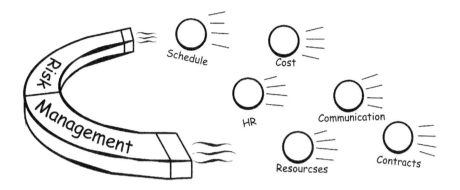

**Risk Management pulls everything together**

The concepts you will learn in risk management can be applied to a variety of subjects. Take for example the concept of prioritization; if you grasp it, you will be able to apply it to many aspects of the business environment.

To be a professional risk manager, you need to distinguish yourself from others. Definitely, you need knowledge; but you also need a set of tools that are unique to risk management, and be able to use them effectively. Think about a professional Porsche mechanic. What distinguishes him from other mechanics is his set of unique wrenches and diagnostic instruments not available to others. Take pride in your profession, and be confident with using risk tools that will be presented in this book. If you find an interesting new tool, do more research about it and try to implement it in your work.

## How This Book Is Different

What distinguishes this work from other books is the framework of study that I propose: to take you gradually from familiarization to memorizing, then to understanding and finally, to application.

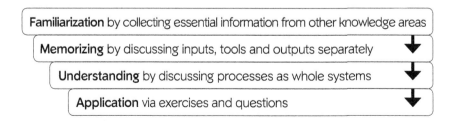

# The Framework of This Book

### The "Memorize then Understand" Framework

I find it difficult to read many PMI exam preparation books. The difficulty is when you have all information cramped together. For example, if you read through the different process and you come across an input, an output or a tool that you are not familiar with, what happens is that - based on my own experience - your thinking momentum just stops, because you go back and forth trying to understand and memorize the new concepts. When this happens, you end up distracted from seeing the whole picture (i.e. the system with all its components). I have divided this book into two parts: the first one focuses on memorizing, while the other focuses on understanding. In this book, I discuss inputs, tools and outputs separately to give you the time to understand and memorize each one of them. Later in the book, I put them all together into what I believe is a logical cohesive whole, in a way that will aid you in passing the exam more easily. I hope this approach will help you to utilize your time more effectively by spending less time on memorizing and more on understanding.

### First, Know the Rules of the Exam

You are choosing to take an exam from the PMI, so invest some time in getting to know how they structure their standards and exams. The Project Management Institute is a non-profit organization that conducts research and sets standards in the field of project management (for more information, visit www.pmi.org). PMI is famous for the Project Management Body of Knowledge (PMBOK® - pronounced P.M.BOK) which is a document of about 400 pages with guidelines on how to initiate, plan, execute, monitor and close a project. The guidelines are a collection of best practices that may or may not apply to all projects- as each project is unique. As I am writing, the fourth update of the PMBOK® is available; so make sure that you get the latest edition.

---

**Suggestion**

- It would be a good idea to register as PMI member because registered members get a free copy of the PMBOK as well as discounts on different PMI books and exams. If you acquire PMI membership and register for the Risk Management Professional exam® (RMP), you will pay less in total than if you register for the exam alone.
- You can download a handbook on the RMP exam from www.pmi.org. You should refer to that handbook to check if the scope and/or duration of the test have changed.

# Introduction

## More on the PMBOK

The PMBOK is the book you need to study for the RMP exam. This study guide is based on the PMBOK to provide you with in-depth explanation of key concepts, examples, illustrations and practice questions helping you to pass the exam without having to consult any other reference. Now let me tell you briefly about the PMBOK. It is an internationally recognized guide on project management and contains the following sections (called "knowledge areas"):

- Integration Management
- Scope Management
- Time Management
- Cost Management
- Quality Management
- Human Resource Management
- Communication Management
- Risk Management
- Procurement Management
- Stakeholders Management

Each of these nine knowledge areas has processes that contain tools. Tools work on certain inputs to produce certain outputs. The knowledge areas are distributed over five project phases: Initiation, Planning, Execution, Monitoring/Control and Closeout. Think of the project phases as the points in time your project is in, and the knowledge areas as the things you do during the phases.

Risk Management is one of the knowledge areas that the PMBOK addresses. It contains six activities (called "processes") which are:

1. Risk Planning
2. Risk Identification
3. Risk Quantitative Assessment
4. Risk Qualitative Assessment
5. Risk Response Planning
6. Risk Monitoring and Control

The distribution of the processes over the project phases is as follows:

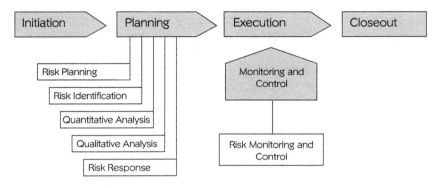

---

**Important**

To answer many questions in the exam, you need to know which process you are currently involved in. For example, if the question says that you are doing Risk Identification, then you are in the planning phase (see diagram above). Exam questions are often put in a more complicated way than this as you may need to use clues from the questions to be able to identify the phase the project is in. For example, if the question mentions that you are using SWOT analysis (a tool in risk identification to be discussed later), this means you are doing risk identification and, thus, the project is in the planning phase. I will give many examples of such in the sample questions but please set your mind from now on to know the "locations" of the processes and their inputs, tools and outputs.

---

**The PMP®**

PMP stands for the famous Project Management Professional certification. The PMP exam covers all the knowledge areas found in the PMBOK. You might wonder if you should take the PMP exam before the RMP exam. Well, I strongly recommend taking the PMP exam but not necessarily before the RMP exam. You can view it from two different perspectives. The RMP exam covers fewer chapters from the PMBOK and thus should be easier to prepare for (for the PMP, you must study the whole PMBOK). On the other hand, the PMP is more famous and also covers Risk Management. It is really a matter of choice.

If you already have a PMP certificate and think you do not need an RMP certificate, I advise you to reconsider. I took the RMP after having achieved my PMP and found the RMP very useful, especially since it made me want to study the subject on "risk" more deeply. Yes, it is all worth it.

**How to Apply for the RMP Exam**

PMI certification is designed more toward recognizing your current status. Surely, there are many new things to learn, but for you to take the exam, you must already have some knowledge and experience in risk management. To be eligible for the exam, you need to do the following:

**Step 1:** Determine if you have the required experience and education. If you have a bachelor's degree, you will need 3,000 hours spent on project risk management, plus 30 hours of training on risk management. If you have a high school diploma, then you will need 4,500 hours of experience and 40 hours of training (visit www.pmi.org for the latest requirements). Your title does not need to be that of a "risk manager" to qualify in the "experience" part, but you need to demonstrate that you worked on some aspects of risk management in your past projects, such as risk identification, communication, etc.

**Step 2:** Register at www.pmi.org by creating a username and password.

**Step 3:** Join the PMI membership and pay the membership fees (this step is optional, but highly recommended).

**Step 4:** Fill in the RMP exam application. The application is available online, and you will need to provide experience and educational information.

**Step 5:** Submit your application through the PMI website. Your application will be reviewed and, once accepted, you will get a reply in a few days with instructions on how to submit payment and schedule your exam.

---

**Suggestion:**

Exam venues and seats are limited per day, so don't delay in scheduling your exam.

---

## What Does the Exam Look Like?

You will have 170 multiple choice questions to answer in three hours and a half. A question can be half a line or a small paragraph with four possible answers (only one is correct). Questions will appear on a computer screen one at a time. The top of the screen will have your name, time remaining and the item number of the question you are answering. Two thirds of the screen will be for the question and its possible answers. At the bottom of the screen, you will have navigation buttons to use to go back and forth through the questions. You will also be able to mark questions so you can return to them later. You will have a built-in calculator that you can use (similar to the one on your PC).

---

**Question 1/170**                                                   **Time remaining 3:15**

**Q:** You are the project Manager of xyz project. Your project is being executed, what Risk Process should you use ?

a) Risk Identification
b) Risk Qualitative Analysis
c) Risk Quantitative Analysis
d) Risk Monitoring and Control

[ Calculator ]

　　　　　　　　　　　Next　　　　Mark　　　Back

---

**Why the Exam Is Difficult**

1. As it is the case with any exam: to pass it, you have to memorize and understand some materials.

2. Duration: It is a long exam (three and a half hours) with many questions.

3. The exam includes some trick questions.

4. For many questions you will be able to eliminate two out of the four multiple choices; but the remaining two choices will be very similar.

Take it as a good thing and as a challenge. You want to be distinguished, so you don't want an exam that just anyone can pass even if he/she is not qualified.

# Chapter 2:
## Essentials

# Essentials

**What You Need to Know to Prepare for the Exam**

Risk management is not an isolated subject. To be a professional risk manager, you need to understand many topics from different areas of knowledge. In this chapter, I collected information that a professional risk manager will use to support his/her job (and thus are potential areas for questions on the exam).

---

During the exam, you will need to perform simple calculations to answer some questions. Statistical concepts are of particular importance in risk management, but don't worry, you need to know only the very basic formulas; like the one for calculating averages.

Remember, there will be a button on the exam screen that enables you to use a calculator similar to the one on your PC. For the calculator, note that:

1. The calculator will be available in all questions; but be careful: not all questions with numbers will require you to use it.

2. Practice using the calculator especially when dealing with percentages and decimal places.

---

## The Risk Model

Risk can be represented mathematically as:

$$\text{Risk} = \text{Probability} * \text{Impact}$$

This mathematical representation (model) should give you a better understanding of the concept of risk and an insight on how it works. The above formula states that risk is the outcome of two parameters: probability and impact. Risk will increase or decrease if any one of them goes up or down, thus, you can control risk (minimize it) by minimizing either probability, impact or both. If you are able to decrease one of the parameters to zero, risk will disappear.

- *Example:*

How do you reduce the risk of a six-year-old girl falling off her bike and breaking a leg?

- *Answer:*

First, write down the risk formula, it will help you to systematically recommend different solutions by either reducing probability, impact or both.

$$\text{Risk} = \text{Probability} * \text{Impact}$$

**Step 1:** Try to reduce the probability of the girl falling. You may do that by educating the girl on how to properly use the bike. An extreme option will be to disallow her from riding the bike, thus eliminating any chance of falling and subsequently any risk of injury.

**Step 2:** Try to reduce the impact by providing her with safety equipment, such as a helmet and padded clothing.

> *Note:*
>
> - *Probability may be referred to as 'chance', 'likelihood', etc.*
>   - *Impact may be referred to as 'severity of the outcome'.*
>   - *Risks can be positive or negative. When a risk is positive, it is called 'opportunity'; when it is negative; it is called a 'threat'.*
>   - *Remember, when we speak about risks, we speak about things that may or may not happen in the future.*

## Matrices

A matrix is a table where the columns and rows represent two variables. It is a visual way of presenting the product of two variables (think of it as a paper calculator). In risk management, we frequently use the Risk Matrix, also known as the 'probability/impact matrix'. In the example below, probabilities are plotted on the vertical line and impacts on the horizontal line. The cells of the table represent the outcome of the multiplication process. Therefore, if the probability is low and impact is high, then their intersection will represent the result of risk. There are nine possible outcomes in the example below, and having a matrix will speed up the process of finding the solution.

Chapter2

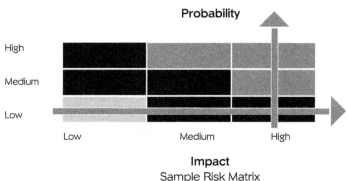

Sample Risk Matrix

Does your company have a risk matrix? How many rows and columns does it have? Check it out.

## **Mean (Average)**

To find the mean of a set of numbers, just add them all and then divide them by their count. Example: for the numbers 2, 3, 4, 9 the mean is 4.5.

$$\text{Mean} = \frac{\text{sum of the given data}}{\text{how many data are given}}$$

$$= \frac{2+3+4+9}{4} = 4.5$$

Finding the average is a simple way of arriving at the expected value from a set of data.

> **Note:** *Don't be too concerned about SD for the exam since there are usually only one or two questions that involve it. However, it would be helpful to have a brief review on the subject.*

## **Standard Deviation (SD)**

Standard deviation will show you how far data are from their mean. In the exam, you might be asked to calculate the standard deviation for a set of numbers and the formula to use is:

$$\text{Standard deviation} = \sqrt{\frac{(\text{sum of each given data-mean})^2}{(\text{the number of data given})}}$$

14

# Essentials

You will not be able to find the SD directly by using the built-in calculator, so you should follow the steps as presented in the example below:

- **Example:**

The standard deviation of 2, 4, 5 and 7 is:

a)   1.802
b)   2.115
c)   1.929
d)   2.005

First, you need to find the mean: [(2 + 4 + 5 + 7) / 4 = 4.5]. Then subtract each number from the mean and multiply the result by itself. It is better to use a table as below:

| Given Number | Mean | Number − mean ( subtract the first two columns, No need to put the minus sign (-) | Find the Square of the answer by multiplying it by itself |
|---|---|---|---|
| 2 | 4.5 | 2.5 | (2.5)*(2.5) = 6.25 |
| 4 | 4.5 | 0.5 | (0.5)*(0.5) = 0.25 |
| 5 | 4.5 | 0.5 | (0.5)*(0.5) = 0.25 |
| 7 | 4.5 | 2.5 | (2.5)*(2.5) = 6.25 |

Now, add the final column and divide the sum by the count number of the given data [(6.25 + 0.25 + 0.25 + 6.25)/(4 ) = 3.25]. Now you need to find the square root of 3.25 but the calculator you have for the exam will not be able to compute it. Here, you will have to work backwards from the given answers by multiplying every answer by itself, which is the reverse process of computing the square root.

| Given Answer | Multiply each Answer by Itself | Compare the result to your final result of 4.33 |
|---|---|---|
| a) 1.802 | 1.802 * 1.802 | 3.25 Correct |
| b) 2.115 | 2.115 * 2.115 | 4.47 Incorrect |
| c) 1.929 | 1.929 * 1.929 | 3.72 Incorrect |
| d) 2.005 | 2.005 * 2.005 | 4.02 Incorrect |

Answer 'a' is correct because multiplying 2.08 by itself gives 3.25, which is the initial answer we got.

## Expected Monetary Value (EMV)

This subject is very important and you should expect quite a few questions involving it. You will be given a monetary value and its chance (probability) of occurring, then you will be asked to find the EMV.

- **Example 1**

You have a 35% chance of generating a $365,000 profit. What is the expected monetary value?

The expected monetary value will be (0.35)*(365,000) = 127,750 dollars

- **Example 2**

There is 15% probability that oil prices will increase by 5% in the course of your construction project, thus costing you $7,625 more in funding. What is the expected monetary value of the increase?

Expected monetary value (0.15)*(7624) = $1,143.6

Note: As you have seen, the expected monetary value can be used for expected profits as well as losses.

## Three-point Estimation

This technique is used to find the expected result from three estimates: a most likely, an optimistic and a pessimistic. To find the expected value, use the following formula:

- **Example:**

$$\text{Expected Value} = \frac{(\text{Best case} + 4 * \text{Most likely} + \text{Worst case})}{6}$$

Find the expected duration for building a car clay prototype from the following information:

Best Case: 43 Hours
Expected: 49 Hours
Worst Case: 62 Hours

- **Answer:**

Expected Time = [43 + (4 * 49) + 62] / 6 = 50.2 hours

> **Note:** The difference between three-point estimation and simply taking the average is that in the former, more weight is given to the most likely result by multiplying it by 4.

## Decision Trees

Decision trees are used when choosing among different options (alternatives). You want to select the option that will cost you less or make you more profit. It is similar to finding the Expected Monetary Value. Just remember, you need to take one option at a time.

- **Example:**

You are the project manager in charge of building a small public clinic. You must subcontract the preparation of the laboratory. You can choose between two contractors. Contractor A will cost you $70,000 and Contractor B will cost you $63,000. However, Contractor A is more famous and has a larger workforce. There is a penalty of $17,000 for delay in preparing the lab. You estimate that Contractor A has a 10% probability of finishing late and Contractor B has a 15% chance of being late. Which contractor should you hire?

**Step 1:** Draw a tree with all the possible options (start from left to right). Write the event name inside a rectangle, and from it, draw all the options. Here, from the first rectangle, we have two options, either to select Contractor A or B. For each of the contractors, we have two possibilities: either a delay happens or does not happen. Write these in new rectangles and add the probabilities on the lines, as shown in the figure next page (Note: The chance of not delaying can be calculated from 100% minus the chance of delay).

# Chapter 2

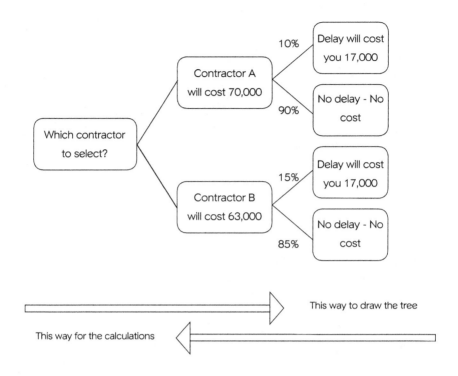

**Step 2:** Now work backwards from right to left and calculate the cost at each rectangle that joins two or more other rectangles. You should use minus (-) signs for the cost but since the whole problem deals with cost (i.e. no mixing of profits and costs), you can do without the minus signs.

**For Contractor A**

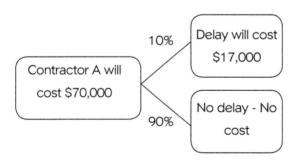

The expected monetary value of hiring Contractor A is its initial cost of $70,000 plus the possible delay cost. We can calculate the cost of delay as follows:

= (Cost of Delay) + (Cost of No Delay)
= (0.1 * 17,000)   + (0.9 * zero)
= $1,700

So, the total cost of hiring contractor A is the initial cost plus the expected delay cost = 70000 + 1700 = 71,700

**For Contractor B**

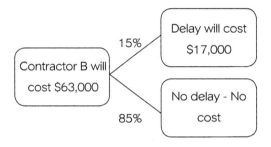

The expected monetary value of hiring Contractor B is the initial cost of $63,000 plus the possible delay cost. We can calculate the cost of delay as follows:

= (Cost of Delay) + (Cost of No Delay)
= (0.15 * 17,000)  + (0.85 * zero)
= $2,550

So, the total cost of hiring Contractor B is the initial cost plus the expected delay cost = $63,000 + $2,550 = $65,550

To solve this problem, remember that you are dealing with cost, not profit, so you need to select the smallest value (cheapest option), which is Contractor B.

> **Note:**
> What if the chance of delay for Contractor B was 60%? If you try to solve the question again, you will find that Contractor A will cost you less in this new scenario.

> **Note:**
> The question can be changed by adding a Contractor C, thus presenting 3 options to choose from.

**Note:**
*If you get a bonus for no delay, it will be money gained. The solution will still follow the same logic but you need to differentiate between profit and loss. For example, what if the Ministry of Health will give you a $1,500 bonus if you finish the lab on time (finishing the lab might be an important milestone in the project). To solve this, you need to be careful which value to add and which to subtract. Let's find the cost of delay for Contractor A which equals the Cost of Delay + Cost of No Delay*

$$= (0.1 * 17,000) + (0.9 * 1500)$$

*Note that the $17,000 is the penalty and the $1,500 is the bonus, so they must be subtracted.*
$$= (\$1700) - (\$1,350) = \$350 \text{ losses}$$

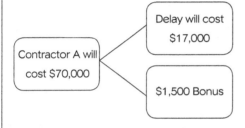

## Earned Value Analysis (EV)

Note: Don't expect to do calculations on Earned Value Management, but you still need to be familiar with it (leave the calculations for the PMP exam).

Earned Value Management (EVM) is a mathematical technique that compares your project execution to your plan (time and cost). EVM links project time to project cost to avoid any misleading interpretations of the project performance. For example, you might be spending less than planned; but that may be due to much less work being done. On the other hand, you might be ahead of schedule because you are overspending. EVM shows your actual progress in the project and helps you identify problems at an early stage. There are sets of formulas you can use for various analyses like:
**CPI** = Cost Performance Index. If the CPI is greater than one (CPI > 1), it indicates that your project is spending less than planned; and if the CPI is less than one (CPI < 1), it means that you are overspending.

# Essentials

**SPI** = Schedule Performance Index. If the SPI is greater than one (SPI > 1), it indicates that your project is ahead of schedule; and if the SPI is less than one (SPI < 1), it means you are behind schedule.

You can also make other calculations like predicting your budget at completion based on your current performance. Earned Value Management is represented by the S-curve (named after its shape). The following figure is a very basic representation of the S-curve.

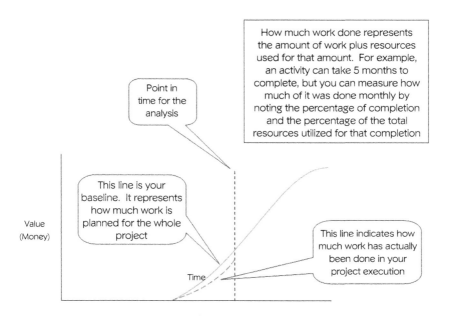

## Modeling and Simulation

*Note:*
*In the exam, you will probably see only a couple of questions on simulation and they tend to be straightforward. Read this section for general information and enjoyment (i.e. don't work too hard trying memorizing everything!).*

Modeling and simulation have many advantages, such as being relatively cheap and giving the chance of testing a large variety of scenarios. Simulation can be very handy and cost effective. Consider an example of studying the effect of waves on the coast of an island. You can use simulation by first building a model. You can build a small pool filled with water and construct a small artificial island. Connect a motor to a piece of plastic that moves up and down to simulate waves. Simulation can be conducted by running the motor at different speeds and observing the effects. The following figure illustrates the model and simulation runs.

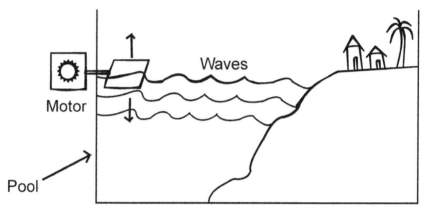

Artificial Waves Model

***Note that our experiment contains the following elements:***

- ***Model***: *Represented by the pool, water and artificial island*
- ***Input Data:*** *You need to determine what setting (speed) to run the motor at.*
- ***Simulation:*** *Running the motor and observing the effects of the artificial waves on the island coast.*

*You will need these elements for risk simulation too. First, we need to build a model of the project using the work breakdown structure and the network diagram. You need to define time, relationships and resources for the project tasks. Then you will have to assign the probability and impact of risks.*

Simulation results will give you the probability (chance) that you will finish exactly on, less or more than what you had budgeted for your project. For example, the result might be that you will have a 68% chance of meeting your project budget of $200,000. Knowing this result will aid you in making an informed decision like re-budgeting.

Simulation is powerful because you can test all your identified risks and their possible outcomes. This is rather a complex task due to the large possibilities associated with risk probabilities and impacts.

To give you a mental image of simulation, consider a software development project were we post the schedule (network diagram) on the floor and ask someone to walk through it. In one hand, he will hold the estimated budget and a stopwatch in the other. He will be required to wait at each task for a time corresponding to the planned duration, and pay the associated cost. When he reaches the finish line, he should have spent the money and time as per the project plan.

Now, for the same network diagram, let's add risks represented by gates (for unplanned delays) and money collectors (for unplanned costs). Also, imagine a very dynamic situation where thousands of people enter the system but with many "what-ifs" representing risks and their impacts. For example: what if the risk happened, what if it did not happen, what if the impact happened as expected, what if the impact was stronger than what was expected, etc.

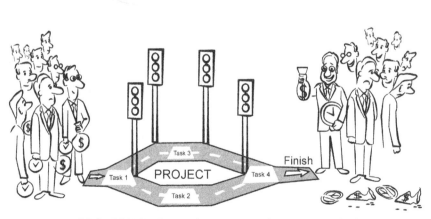

PROJECT SIMULATION RUN ( INCLUDING RISKS)

In the above illustration, note that at the end, people are either happy or sad, representing successful or unsuccessful project completion. If we have 1,000 people going through the model and only 300 coming out with money left in their hand (or did not borrow), then we have a 30% chance of finishing within budget. Simulation makes us explore all the "what-ifs" in a fast and organized manner.

In the exam, expect questions on simulation to be superficial; such as questions that assess one's knowledge of the definition, but I hope that after you pass the exam, you will invest more time in learning more about risk simulation.

## ■ Monte Carlo Simulation

Monte Carlo is a technique (formula) used to generate numbers as inputs for simulation. Instead of using a single number (like the most likely estimate), we use all possible estimates (by using a distribution), and thus be able to get all possible outcomes. For example, if you estimate the new price of cement to be about $5 per bag but not less than $4 and not more than $6.2, then it is justified to use $5 (or better yet, compute the expected value using the three-point estimation). However, in Monte Carlo Simulation, we will use ALL the numbers between 4 and 6.2. Not only that, we will also use the numbers in respect to their chance of happening, meaning that we will use more data close to the most likely price of $5 than to the lowest and highest. So distribution is just an interval of numbers organized on their chance of occurrence, and the beauty of using Monte Carlo is that you use a set of expected numbers instead of a single most likely estimate, thus increasing accuracy.

There are different kinds of distributions you can use in your Monte Carlo simulation and they are discussed later in this chapter.

---

Monte Carlo is a very interesting subject, but for the exam, remember that:

- Monte Carlo is used to generate random numbers in simulation
- It is often called Monte Carlo simulation
- Monte Carlo helps reduce uncertainty
- Monte Carlo uses probability distributions

---

Before you proceed, make sure that the statement below makes sense:

For simulation, you need to first build a model. To run a simulation, you need input data. Input data will be generated by the Monte Carlo technique. Monte Carlo is a formula and needs a distribution to generate numbers based on their likelihood of occurrence. Once the simulation is completed, you will have many output data that require analysis. Simulation is usually done using computers.

**Risk Simulation**

## Probability Distribution

Distribution represents a range of numbers and their chances of occurrence. For the exam, it might be enough to remember the names of the distributions and their properties, but I will give more information to help you understand them. The following are different types of famous distributions:

- **Triangular Distribution**

This distribution is used when we can estimate three numbers for an event: a most likely, upper and lower limit. Use this distribution when you don't have experimental data, but only opinions of experts in the field. An example of using triangular distribution is if you want to simulate how long it will take you to get to work from your home. From experience, you can say that: I will probably take 25 minutes getting to work, but not less than 20, and not more than 31.

The following are illustrations of the distribution where the first figure represents a symmetrical triangular distribution and the second represents an asymmetrical one.

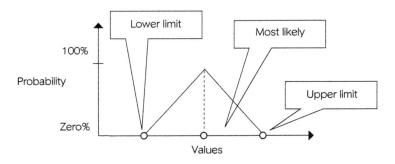

**Symmetrical Triangular Distribution**

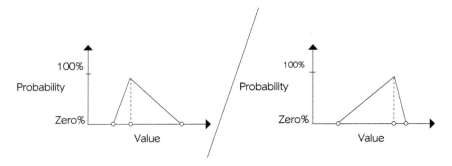

**Asymmetrical Triangular Distribution**

This distribution is used frequently in simulation because it is relatively easy to create from the judgment of experts. It also provides a better estimation than uniform distribution because the 'most likely' data to occur have more weight (importance) than the other data.

- **Uniform Distribution**

You can use it when you know a minimum and a maximum value but no value in between has a greater chance of occurring than another.

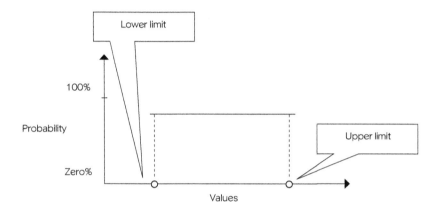

- **Beta Distribution**

Like the triangular distribution, beta distribution gives more weight to the most likely value. Beta distribution can also be asymmetric, being skewed to the left or right. Beta distribution is sometimes called PERT distribution for its frequent use in project simulations using the PERT network diagram.

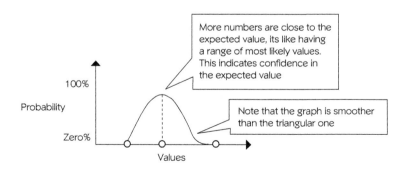

- **Normal Distribution**

Also called the "bell shaped" distribution. This distribution resembles many real life facts (like the height of people) where majority of the results are close to the average(s) (think about it, most people in your work area are close or similar in height).

- **Lognormal Distribution**

This distribution is a special form of the normal distribution and frequently used for reliability applications like those on equipment failure.

## Sensitivity Analysis

Sensitivity here is concerned with identifying risks that have the biggest impact on the project, and thus require more attention. Example: a project is more sensitive to work done by Subcontractor A than to that done by Subcontractor B, simply because Subcontractor A handles work that is more critical. Knowing that, you will put more controls on that subcontractor (a good place to put controls is in the contract document).

Consider the example where you use steel, cement, wood and diesel in your construction project. You made a sensitivity analysis on the risk of price increase in each one of these items and found the following:

- $1 increase in the price of steel will lead to a project budget increase of $4,500
- $1 increase in the price of cement will lead to a project budget increase of $7,000
- $1 increase in the price of wood will lead to a project budget increase of $3,750
- $1 increase in the price of diesel will lead to a project budget increase of $3,500

From the above, you figure out that risks of cement prices increase can affect your project the most. You may then decide to buy all the cement you need for your project in advance (but then, you will need storage space! Its really quite complicated, especially in the real world).

# Essentials

The figure below is for a Tornado Diagram, which visually represents risk sensitivity and arranges risks based on their impact (you can have different tornado diagrams for cost, time, etc.).

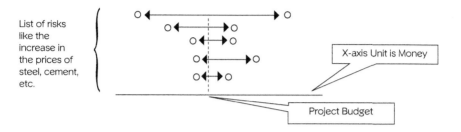

---

For the exam, remember that:

- Sensitivity analysis prioritizes risks based on their potential impacts on the project.
- The tornado diagram is a graphical representation of sensitivity analysis.
- Sensitivity analysis can be done for different parameters like cost and schedule.
- In the exam, you will not be required to make calculations on sensitivity; however, know that to find sensitivity for an element you need to FIX all other elements.

---

## Contract Types

Risks in your project may be generated or controlled by the type of contract you use. There are two famous contract types (and a hybrid of both):

■ **Fixed Price Contract:** Here, as a sponsor, you will pay a fixed amount of money to get your desired output. In this type, more risks are put on the seller (contractor) as he will need to finish the project at the specified cost even if he faces unplanned events; such as increase in material costs. However, this type of contract usually costs more as the seller will add a risk margin to cover anticipated risks. For this type, the buyer (sponsor) should be very specific on the desired output.

■ **Cost Reimbursable Contract:** Here the seller gets paid the cost of doing the job plus a profit margin. More risks are present on the buyer's part. For example, if material costs increase, he will incur the cost. This type of contract is more flexible as it allows for changes more easily.

- **Time and Materials Contract:** This type has elements from the two types previously discussed. It allows you to start the project before finalizing the scope but sets limits on some parameters like the cost of certain materials used.

## Baselines

A baseline is a plan created during the project planning phase. An example is your schedule plan which will be your baseline (benchmark) against which you will compare your actual project performance. Famous project baselines are for time, cost and quality.

## Assumptions

When we assume, we are basically confident that something will happen without having prior evidence. Our life will be difficult without assumptions, as if we stop to assume, then we need to investigate and give a reason for everything. However, our assumptions should be reasonable and derived from our experience and knowledge. Examples of assumptions in a project are:

- There will be no thunderstorms during the project
- The project manager will not get seriously injured in a car accident
- Oil prices will not increase by more than $3 per barrel during the project
- There will be no strikes in the airport to affect a major meeting

For your project, it is a good idea to log your assumptions in a document so you will be able to think about them (or maybe ask other people to comment on them). In addition, if you log your assumptions, you can update them during the different stages in your project. When you make assumptions, you have to be reasonable and avoid going to extremes. For example, it is perfectly fine to assume that it will not snow in the middle of your construction project in the desert. However, it is unreasonable to assume that a shipment delivery will not be delayed.

Essentials

From my experience, the single most dangerous assumption in projects deals with information transfer, where you assume that your message is received and understood correctly as intended.

## Network Diagram/PERT/CPM

The Network Diagram/PERT/CPM are similar techniques for representing your project graphically. The representation shows the relationships between tasks and their duration. The diagrams will be helpful for you in risk management especially in risk identification and simulation. The following is an example of a network diagram:

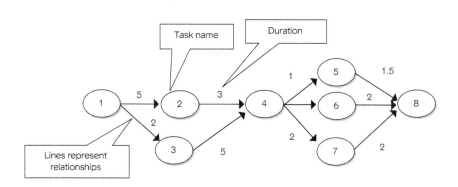

## Work Breakdown Structure (WBS)

The Work Breakdown Structure (WBS) is one of the first things you need to do after defining the project scope. In it, you will include all the activities needed to complete a project. You can use it to add time, resources and relationships between tasks. In addition, WBS can be a great communication tool for communicating what the project is meant to accomplish.

To create a WBS, you need to break down your project in stages, where, at each stage, you introduce more details. Start at the top with the main deliverable of the project and work your way down until you reach a basic level of tasks with which you can comfortably associate money and time. A WBS can take many shapes and styles; the following style is widely used:

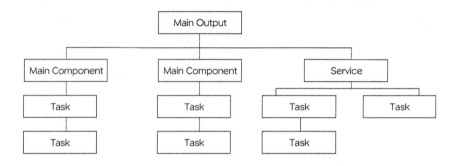

- *Exercise*

Make a WBS for a "project" on a trip to attend a project management conference in Finland:

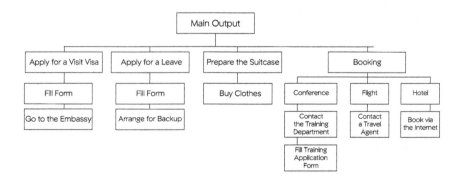

Essentials

> *Note:* WBS is frequently defined as a hierarchical representation of project tasks. Also, in the PMBOK, the tasks that are lowest in the hierarchy are referred to as "work packages". Work packages are tasks to which you can clearly assign time and resources.

## Gantt Chart

The Gantt chart is a time graph of the project. It is widely used for project scheduling and shows when tasks will start and how long they will take.

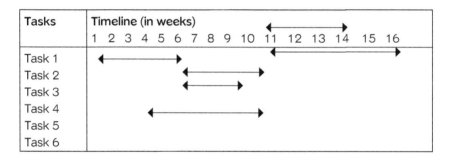

## Quality Tools

In the multiple choices in the exam, you might see some quality tools mixed with risk tools to trick you. Here, I have briefly discussed some of the tools so you are not tricked into making the wrong choices in the exam. You don't need to spend a lot of time on them, but if you are personally interested, you can refer to the quality chapter in the PMBOK for more information.

33

# Chapter2

## ■ Control Charts

A control chart is a graph that plots an outcome graphically to see if the outcome is within specified limits (i.e. is the activity under control and headed toward the intended direction?).

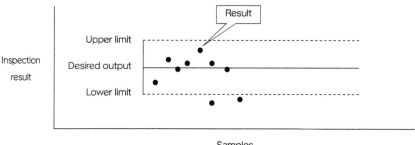

## ■ Histogram

A histogram is a graphical representation of which situation/event occurs (happens) with the most frequency. It is like writing all possible events on a piece of paper and then, for each time an event happens, you put a coin over it.

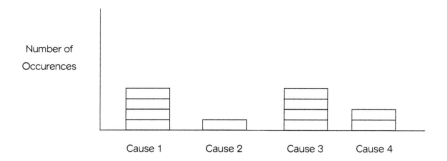

## Pareto Analysis/Law or the 20/80 Rule

For the exam, know that the Pareto Analysis law states that 80% of all occurrences are caused by only 20% of all possible causes.

> **Note:** This concept is named after an Italian economist who found that 80% of the land in Italy was owned by only 20% of the people.

## Scatter Diagram

The scatter diagram is a plot of two variables showing a relationship between them. The relationship (if it exists) can be guessed by noting how data are scattered.

> There are other quality tools, but don't expect any direct questions about them in the exam, just be familiar with them and their general description.

## Leadership Styles

People working on projects can be a source of risk(s). Imagine being the project manager where your team is composed of fresh graduates with no work experience. How will this affect your project?

- **Autocratic Leadership**

In autocratic leadership style, the leader has (and exercises) high levels of influence and control over his/her team. Members of the team are not encouraged to make suggestions. Risks that arise from this style are lack of creativity, low morale and low commitment.

- **Charismatic Leadership**

In the charismatic leadership style, the leader has enough charm to make people follow him/her even without formal authority (you know, the people everyone likes and listens to). A typical charismatic leader is energetic and can easily convince his/her team to follow his/her lead. Risks in this style lie in the tendency of turning the project into a "one man show" where, if the leader leaves, the team output decreases. The commitment given is not intended for the project goals but more so toward the leader.

- **Laissez-faire Leadership**

In the laissez-faire leadership style, the leader gives his/her team enough space for creativity and innovation. The leader does not practice strong and excessive control over his/her team because they are knowledgeable and experienced. The term is French and means to "let do".

### ■ Democratic Leadership

In the democratic leadership style, the leader invites the team to "participate" in decision-making. This usually yields better participation and more creative ideas than in an autocracy but also tends to take more time when it comes to decision-making.

### ■ People-Oriented Leadership

In people-oriented leadership style, the leader focuses on coaching and helping his team members. In this style, risks can generate because the leader might over-focus on the people's side while giving less attention to the tasks to be accomplished.

### ■ Task-Oriented Leadership

Here, the leader focuses almost entirely on meeting objectives, with little or no concern for the team's satisfaction. What negative effect would this style have on a team?

### ■ Bureaucratic Leadership

As the name suggests, a bureaucratic leader strictly follows procedures and leaves little or no place at all for flexibility (no breaking of the rules). Can you guess the risks this style poses on a project team?

### . *Exercise*

Connect each leadership style with the item that better describes its attributes:

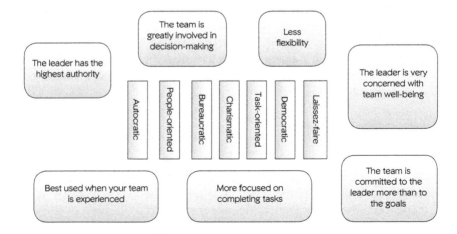

## Motivation Theories

As mentioned earlier, people can be a source of risk(s). In many projects, you will encounter people with low morale and commitment, and they can negatively affect the project. For the exam, you might encounter some questions about motivation theories. Below are descriptions of some.

- **Maslow's Hierarchy of Needs**

This is a very famous theory. Abraham Maslow suggests that for a human being to reach his/her full potential, there are needs that have to be satisfied. For example, your construction workers will not be fully motivated if they get only four hours of sleep. You can use the theory in gap analysis to identify why a team member is not performing well or as expected. The theory is represented in the famous pyramid (you don't need to remember what is inside the pyramid, but it is really worth pondering upon).

- **McGregor's Theory of X&Y**

This theory groups workers into two types:

Theory X: Suggests that people do not like work and responsibility. Thus, managers need to practice close monitoring and control and direction is needed.

Theory Y: Suggests that people like to work and take responsibility. Thus, managers need to involve them and give them "more space".

### ■ Herzberg's Theory

The Herzberg's theory is also called the motivation hygiene or the two-factor theory. Here, you have factors that contribute to satisfaction and factors that contribute to dissatisfaction. Herzberg argues that the more satisfied an employee is, the more motivated he/she will be.

## Organizational Structure

Expect some questions on this area. Organizational structures are about who has control over the staff and resources and how communication flows. The type of structure can generate risks, especially in communication. Try to understand the materials presented here, and identify the advantages and disadvantages of each structure. Don't try to remember the disadvantages/ advantages word for word (remember, you will have a multiple-choice exam, not a fill-in-the-blanks one). To help you differentiate among the structures, know that the project manager is happiest in a projectized structure, because he/she has more control over resources and authority over the project team, and saddest in a functional one because of lack of authority.

### 1- Functional Structure

This structure is frequently found in many organizations and governmental entities. Disciplines are organized in separate areas (see figure below). Organizations with this structure have more control on processes but tend to be slow in internal activities due to a rigid structure of responsibilities and communications.

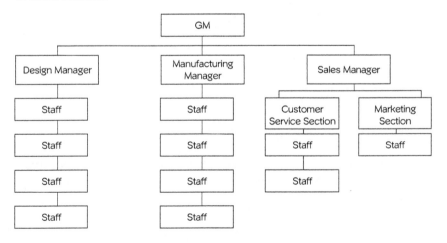

Sample of a Functional Structure

Consider a project to build a chair in a furniture manufacturing setup. The project might start at the manufacturing unit with a selected project manager and team from the manufacturing division. When the skills of a designer are needed, a formal request will be sent from the manager of manufacturing to the manager of design to provide the needed services.

The following table summarizes the advantages and disadvantages of the functional structure.

| Advantages | Disadvantages |
|---|---|
| • Clear roles of staff<br>• Clear communication channels<br>• Staff are given the opportunity to improve their field experience and knowledge<br>• Clear promotion path for staff | • Staff give priority to their day-to-day work, not on project work<br>• Projects are confined to a single unit and input from others is not efficiently delivered (due to long communication channels) |

- Workers = ☺
- Project Manager = ☹

## 2 - Projectized Structure

You can view this as the opposite of a functional structure. Here the project manager has full authority on the project team. In this setup, the project team is fully dedicated to the project, and once the project is finished, they are taken to accomplish another. Organizations with this structure are more dynamic. An example is a TV news channel, where being fast and flexible is important.

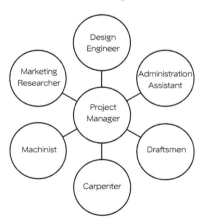

Sample of a Projectized Structure

The following table summarizes the advantages and disadvantages of a projectized structure (from a project management perspective).

| Advantages | Disadvantages |
|---|---|
| • Staff gives priority to the project<br>• Project manager has control over the resources and staff<br>• Mixed knowledge and experience within the team | • Duplication of staff in different projects<br>• workers might feel a lack of security as they can be dismissed after the completion of the project |

- Workers = ☺ (they are less happy than in a functional structure)
- Project Manager = ☺

### 3 - Matrix Organization

A matrix structure is a mix of the previous two structures. It aims at collecting as many benefits as possible for a project administration. In the matrix, the functional structure is maintained but a project manager has some control on the resources and has formal authority over the staff from different functional units. See the figure below and you may be able to guess the advantages of the matrix, especially in providing more channels of communication.

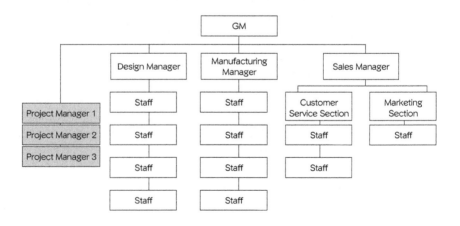

Example of a Matrix Organization

# Essentials

The matrix structure can be strong, weak or balanced, depending on the project manager's extent of authority. The stronger the authority is, the stronger the matrix structure is supposed to be. You can think of functional organizations as having a weak matrix and projectized organizations as having a very strong matrix.

The following table summarizes the advantages and disadvantages of a matrix structure (from a project management perspective).

| Advantages | Disadvantages |
| --- | --- |
| • Staff are more committed to the project, where their functional manager allows them to make time for project work<br>• Less resource duplication<br>• Better communication channels | • The main disadvantage is the difficulty to manage people in this setup because they are expected to meet both functional and project requirements (they have 2 bosses, the Project Manager and the Functional Manager) |

- **Exercise:**

Knowing the different organizational structures is important for the exam. To check your understanding, accomplish the following exercises, and if you find them easy, you may not need to go over the structures again.

**Question 1:** For each organizational structure, connect the advantages and disadvantages:

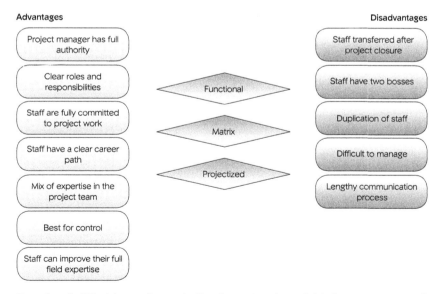

**Question 2:** What type of organizational structure is available in your company?

# Chapter 3:
# Communication & Stakeholders Managment

# Communication & StakeholdersManagment

As much as one third of the exam will be on risk communication. Communication is a soft and straightforward concept; but if you do not believe in it, you will have difficulty answering the exam, because many questions are situational and ask you to decide on the BEST course of action.

## Stakeholders

"Stakeholders" - expect to see this word repeated in the exam as many times as you see the word "risk". Communication in your project should be mostly about managing the stakeholders. Every project will have its unique stakeholders whom you need to identify. Stakeholders are entities who have interests in your project, such as the project team, sponsor, the public, governmental authorities, the client, subcontractor, etc. The project sponsor is one of the most important stakeholders, because the sponsor is the one who provides the financial resources. Stakeholders can affect the project and the project can affect them as well. These effects can be positive or negative.

The project team is responsible for identifying the stakeholders and their requirements. Stakeholders too have responsibilities; the most important of which are to participate in the project meetings and communicate their concerns in a timely manner.

Stakeholders and communication management are sometimes taken for granted or neglected in projects. If you believe in these concepts, you will do well in this part even with just a little study. Unfortunately, I have seen many people who are able to speak about the importance of stakeholders for hours and hours in meetings, but when it comes to implementation, they do not let that spoken of importance reflect. When they refer to stakeholders in real life examples, they use words like: "they don't need to know", "they must accept it", "why should I send them this information", etc.

## How NOT to go Wrong with Stakeholders?

- Be active not reactive (you invite them, call them and reach out to them)
- You need to identify them (every project has its unique stakeholders, don't just copy and paste the list from your last project)

# Communication & Stakeholders

- Rank their level of power and interest to influence the project
- Collect their requirements
- Invite them to participate in meetings, brainstorming sessions, etc.
- Give attention to them and incorporate their requirements in line with project objectives
- Make sure that you include them in the communication plan and share information with them
- Look into their issues (don't ignore them)
- Adopt a "win-win" strategy
- Understand that they have different interests and what might be important to one might be trivial to another

*. Exercise:*

Can you give an example of stakeholders who affected a project positively or negatively? Can you think of an example involving environmental activists?

*Back to Communication*

To have effective communication in your project, you need a plan called a 'communication plan'. This plan will include what will be communicated, to whom it will be communicated and when it will be communicated.

The table below shows a sample communication plan; see how simple it can be.

| WHAT INFORMATION | TO WHOM | HOW | FREQUENCY |
|---|---|---|---|
| Weekly meeting minutes | Project team | Meetings + Reports | Weekly |
| Monthly progress reports | All | Presentations + Reports | Monthly |
| Risk register updates | Project team + Sponsor + Stakeholders A and C | Word document attached in e-mails | As needed |
| Post project review | ALL + Project Management Office | Meetings + Reports | At project end |

You will have to do some work before making the communication plan. The most important thing to do is to identify the stakeholders and to log them in a stakeholders register.

> **Note:** Don't confuse the communication plan with the stakeholders register. The plan gives you a picture of how communication will take place, while the register holds stakeholders' information; i.e. their names, contact numbers, e-mails, etc.

## Communication Basics

Communication is the process of sending information between two or more people. Communication is quite often infected with misunderstandings. Let's draw a communication model and see the possible causes of misunderstandings. The model consists of:

- **Sender**: The person initiating the communication by sending a message
- **Receiver**: The person or people receiving the message
- **Message**: Usually verbal, but can also be in the form of signs and gestures or be written
- **Medium**: The way a message is being sent and with what technology (e.g. voice, picture, advertisement, phone, internet, etc.)

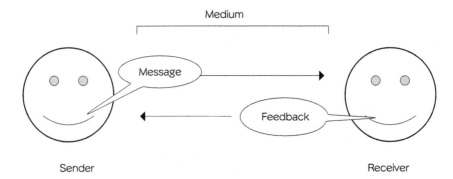

Now, let us see the lifecycle of a message and what can go wrong as illustrated in the table below.

| Stage | Description | What Can Go Wrong |
|---|---|---|
| 1 | Message Creation | • Ambiguous tone of voice/body language<br>• Speaking in a language other than your mother tongue<br>• Lack of mastery of technical terminology (jargon) that leads to the poor expression of one's thoughts and ideas<br>• Fear (example: when talking to your boss or the GM) |
| 2 | Message Transfer | • Not selecting the right medium (like discussing drawings over the phone or sending an attachment that requires a special software to open)<br>• Problem with the medium (like physical noise when using voice or poor cell phone coverage) |
| 3 | Message Reception and Interpretation (Decoding) | • Receiver's emotional, mental or physical state (such as being angry or tired)<br>• Language mastery<br>• Terminology mastery |

As you can see, many factors can negatively affect the communication process; such factors are called communication blockers. A very effective way of drastically improving communication is by providing feedback from the receiver to the sender where he/she repeats what was understood from the message.

When you speak, both the volume and pitch of your voice tone and the body language are responsible for transferring more than 90% of your message and the rest depend on the actual message content. You should never neglect your tone of voice and body language, since they can block communication if others perceive the message - and consequently, yourself - as disrespectful or aggressive. This is particularly important when working on a multicultural project. Many companies try to be more proactive in this regard, and when undertaking projects in other countries, they give their staff an introductory course on the local culture of the country where the project will be. An example of the importance of cross-cultural literacy is that of a US executive who is sent to manage a project in a subsidiary in Japan. There are many differences in management styles between the two countries, which can cause conflicts, misunderstandings and, ultimately, project failure. An example of such management style differences is the decision-making process where the American style is more toward individuals making the decisions and being accountable for it while the Japanese style is toward decisions made by groups with shared accountability.

## Communication Methods, Technology and Dimensions

I will discuss some fundamentals of communication below. We always practice these fundamentals even without thinking about them. They seem to come naturally, although in fact, we learn them throughout the life course. Being able to identify them will not only help you to answer more questions correctly but will also make you think about communication in a different way.

### Communication Methods

You can communicate with stakeholders in different ways. Such ways are referred to as communication methods. These methods are:

- **The Interactive Method:** This is the best way to communicate because both parties are sending and receiving information, thus allowing opportunities for clarification. Interactive communication is usually done face-to-face but also can be done via video conferencing and telephones.

- **The Pull Method:** In this context, the project manager makes all information available and accessible in a designated resource center or venue and the stakeholder(s) "pull" the data as needed. For example, the project manager might make the information available via a server or a secretariat. Can you think of risks associated with this method? Will all stakeholders be motivated to make the effort to get the information?

- **The Push Method:** This is the opposite of the pull method. In this method, the project team pushes (sends) information onto the stakeholders. This is often done via email attachments and memos. Here, you have the risk of information being lost in transition; however, you can make a system to track delivery.

## Communication Technology

Once you decide on the method of communication, you need to figure out which is the best tool to apply your method. If you need to have interactive communication but your project is physically spread over hundreds of miles, then you can choose video conferencing, but how costly will it be? and is it available in different areas of the project? Also, you might use email to send AutoCAD® drawings, but you have to make sure that all recipients are able to open them, or else send such files in Adobe® PDF format.

## Dimensions of Communication

There are many types of communication. Our brains automatically select different styles for different situations. However, actively thinking about the styles and when to use them will give you the advantage of better preparation and consistency. As per the PMBOK, you can use the following styles in project communication:

| Dimension | Usage |
| --- | --- |
| Internal | For communication within the project |
| External | Done with other departments in the organization, governmental entities, media, suppliers, etc. |
| Formal | Verbal: Presentation to the management<br>Written: Reports like progress reports, change requests, memos, etc. |
| Informal | Emails, day-to-day verbal discussions, etc. |
| Horizontal | With colleagues and peers |
| Vertical | With your boss (up) or your staff (down) |

## Communication Channels

To ensure proper communication, you need to spend a lot of effort. To show you how complex communication can be in a project, there is a formula to calculate possible communication channels (how many "who can talk with whom"). The formula is where **n** is the number of people. Therefore, if you have seven people, then the number of possible communication routes between them is 7(7-1)/2 = 21. You should remember the formula in case you encounter a direct question about it in the exam. However, you might get confused about it, for example, you may forget whether it is (n+1) or (n-1). There is a trick that can help you. First, manually find the number of channels for a simple situation, like one involving four people, as follows:

Count the lines and you will know that for four people you have six channels. Use this information to validate your formula by plugging the numbers, and once you are confident about the formula, you can use it to solve any question about the number of communication channels.

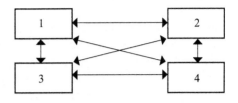

## Communication Skills

Knowing how to communicate might be the single most important soft skill. I will not spend time discussing its importance, but I will say that, sadly, if you ask many managers to list communication skills in an exam, he/she may do very well but in real life, there is a lack of practice. Expect some questions about communication skills where you will be asked to decide which skill to use in a problematic situation (most likely, a conflict between stakeholders). Here is a list of some of these communication skills.

- **Listening**: Everyone benefits from listening. We should listen to understand and not to "catch" mistakes. Active listening is a great tool to build trust with and within your project team and stakeholders. Personally, I have found that active listening is all that you need to solve many conflicts. Think about it, when you had conflicts with your parents when you were a teenager, all that you wanted was just to have them listen to you.

- **Negotiation**: When you negotiate, it is better to do it face-to-face and aim for a win-win situation. Always be respectful of others and be prepared with relevant documents and proofs.

- **Conflict Resolution:** Usually, you will see conflicts arising between or among stakeholders and within the project team. First, you need to identify conflicts from the beginning and act immediately to prevent them from escalating and affecting your project. You need to understand conflicts and the true (basic) reasons behind them. You need to build trust between parties which will help you to promote a win-win solution.

### Moving Back to Stakeholders

Communication and stakeholder management are strongly related. Stakeholder management is how you put communication into practice.

## Stakeholder Identification (The Stakeholder Register)

You need to identify stakeholders so you can communicate with them effectively. To identify stakeholders, we use techniques like brainstorming and expert judgment.

> **Note:** The stakeholder register can be a simple table with the stakeholder's name, contact details and requirements. The register will be updated many times as more information becomes available. After identifying the stakeholders, you need to find their expectations and make a strategy to manage those expectations. All this information should be included in the register.

## Stakeholder Classification ( Analysis )

Chances are that you will have many stakeholders in your project. However, you do not need to manage them in the same way. You need to balance your resources and the project scope with their expectations. To classify stakeholders, consider the following techniques:

> **Note:** This is a rather interesting subject, but don't expect complex or difficult questions about it in the exam.

- **Power/Interest Grid**

Here, you simply assign a score (high or low) to each stakeholder based on:

**Power:** The ability of a stakeholder to influence your project, either positively or negatively.

**Interest:** How interested is the stakeholder in actually using his/her power in the project?

What is in it for him/her? How much is at stake?
You can use a matrix to group the stakeholders as follows:

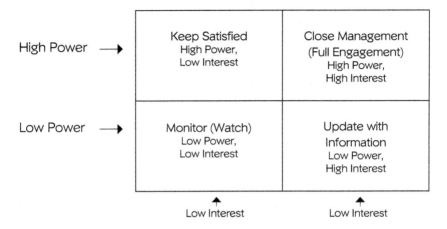

You can manage each stakeholder based on his/her location in the matrix. According to the PMBOK, you can monitor, keep informed, keep satisfied or closely manage a stakeholder (see the figure above).

---

- Other grids can be used; such as the power/influence grid and influence/impact grid, however, they all have the same concept.
- Here is an idea for you, if you are good at MS® Excel, you can make a file that will automatically plot stakeholders in a grid after assigning their level of power and interest. Then share your file on the Internet and email me a copy.

---

### ■ Salience

This is another way to group stakeholders. The concept is similar to the above technique but has three levels of evaluation: power, legitimacy and urgency. This will result in grouping stakeholders into eight categories. The naming of the groups is very interesting. You will have, for example, a "dangerous" stakeholder (one who has power and urgency but no legitimacy) and a "demanding" stakeholder (one who has only urgency). I believe that this subject is worth devoting more time to, but, for now, knowing that the name salience refers to stakeholder analysis might be enough for the exam.

# Communication & Stakeholders

# Chapter 4:
# Introduction to Risk Management

# Introduction to Risk Management

Let's start talking about risks from the perspective of the RMP exam. First, let us discuss two essential concepts: risk management and the input/output process.

**Risk Management** is something that we always do even without thinking about it. Consider the following example:

Risk Identification      Risk Assessment      Risk Control

Above is a very simple example of the risk management process. First, a potential harm is identified, then an assessment of the possible damage is done (sometimes in the blink of an eye); finally, action is taken to control the risk. Make sure that you are comfortable with the idea that when we discuss risks, we are speaking about the future (in the example above, nobody actually tripped on the cable).

Introduction to Risk Management

Input/Output Processes

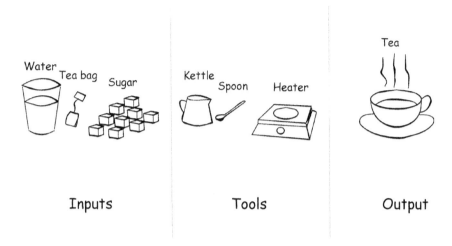

For the exam, you need to SET your mind to think in terms of inputs/outputs and tools. The concept of process is straightforward and is illustrated above in the steps of the tea-making example. In risk management, you are dealing with information, so your inputs, outputs and tools are usually documents and mind-techniques.

For the exam, you need to know with absolute certainty in which stage of the process you are in to be able to answer many of the questions. You can identify your location among the processes indirectly by knowing which input, output or tool you are dealing with. For example, if you are using a spoon then you know that you are in the second stage of the tea-making process (see the illustration above).

## The Risk Management Processes

Risk management is one of the nine knowledge areas that the PMBOK addresses. Risk management involves six processes. The processes are logical and you shouldn't have difficulty understanding and memorizing their sequence. For each process, there are tools, inputs and outputs. Some inputs, outputs and even tools are used repeatedly in different processes, and the most important output by far is the Risk Register.

The following table gives a summary of the different risk management processes:

| Process | Description |
|---|---|
| Risk Planning | This is the process where you define a "road map" for risk management. You will specify what is needed, what tools will be used and who will be involved. |
| Risk Identification | In this process, you will use different tools to come up with a list of risks that might occur in the project. |
| Risk Qualitative Assessment | Arranges the risks you have identified, from most important to least important. |
| Risk Quantitative Assessment | Tests how the risks may affect the project (using mathematical formulas and computers). |
| Risk Response Planning | Strategies that are used to control the risks. Controlling the risks will most likely affect your schedule and cost plans. |
| Risk Monitoring and Control | This process is done during the project execution phase. You monitor and audit risks, identify new ones and issue change requests as needed. |

The figure below maps out the different risk management processes to the project management phases.

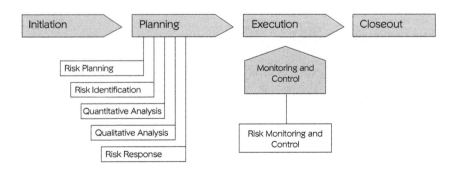

> **Note** that all the risk processes take place during project planning phase except for risk monitoring and control, which take place during project execution. However, during execution new risks are often identified, so you need to repeat some of the risk processes.

## How Not to Forget the Processes

Everyone has his own way of remembering people, places, objects and the like, by associating names with pictures. Below is a method I have used to make sure that I don't forget the PMI risk management processes:

1. I start with the 3 basic processes in risk management that I remember very well: identification, assessment and response.
2. I also remember that they are six processes in total.
3. For risk assessment, I know that there are two types: qualitative and quantitative, so I expand risk assessment to the two processes.
4. Now, I have four processes, and to make them six, I add one process at the beginning and one at the end. The one at the beginning is the preparation (i.e. planning) part and the one at the end involves checking your work (i.e. monitoring and control).

> *Note:*
> *Memorize the names and sequence of the six processes before you proceed to the next chapter.*

## When to Start Risk Management?

PMBOK has ten knowledge areas. Risk management comes at the end of the project planning stage, because, for risk management, you need input from other knowledge areas. The table in the next page gives you what other knowledge areas in the PMBOK contribute to risk management:

| Knowledge Area | Contribution to Risk Management |
| --- | --- |
| Scope Management | What is included in the project and what is not |
| Time Management | Work breakdown structure and schedule baseline |
| Cost Management | Cost baseline and budgeting |
| Quality Management | Quality standards and specifications required for the project |
| Human Resource Management | Organizational chart, project team members, staff availability, etc. |
| Communication & Stakeholders Management | Know the stakeholders and their expectations, and the communication plan |

*Note: You don't have to memorize this table.*

The only knowledge area that is planned after risk management is procurement management, because you often need to include clauses to manage specific risks in your projects. This only becomes clear after risk response planning. For example, if you decide that the contractor should be responsible for risks that may occur due to expected new legislations, then this must be spelled out in the agreement with the contractor.

Having said the above, you need to understand that in real life a project doesn't unfold in a step after step fashion. You will ultimately need to go back and forth between the different knowledge areas.

# Introduction to Risk Management

# Chapter 5:
## Inputs/Outputs

# Inputs/Outputs

**Structure of This Chapter**

This chapter is different. Unlike other PMI exam books, I will discuss all inputs, outputs and tools separately from their processes. I have done that because when I was studying for the exam, I often had to stop reading and usually got distracted since unfamiliar tools, inputs or outputs kept popping up at one stage or another. This in turn slowed my studying momentum and made me lose sight of the processes as a whole system.

By discussing components separately from the whole process, you will be able to focus on understanding them, and, if there is a need, to memorize them, you may do so without the additional task of having to know how they fit together. This will, in turn, decrease distraction when you study the complete process (in the next chapters), and hopefully, will make you more confident as you will not be distracted by the popping-up of unfamiliar concepts.

Study this chapter carefully as the largest portion of the exam questions will be based on concepts that are discussed here.

## Tools

### 1 - Tools for Risk Planning

- **Planning Meetings**

These are meetings conducted to formulate a plan/ plans. The project manager discuss with his/her team HOW to do risk management (e.g. what method and techniques to use). To make your meetings effective, you need to prepare for them, select a good venue and invite all concerned stakeholders.

- **Expert judgment :** if your plan is filled with error and wrong assumptions you will face trouble implementing it. Thus you should consult with people who have experience in the topics it will cover. For example, your risk plan will include roles and responsibilities and senior management can help you decide on that. Also, you need to include the approved forms to be used for risk management activities. People in your risk department or project management office will provide them and might help you to customize them.

- **Analytical techniques:** consider this example: there are two families planning to go on a vacation. One family will go for a Safari in a remote area in Africa and the second will go to London. The first family have a young 2 years old boy and the second have two teenaged daughters. Now, if I asked you this in the exam: which family will need to plan for stronger risk management. Without thinking you will say "family number one". But you didn't come to this correct answer without thinking. Very fast in your mind you analyzed that since family one will be in a remote area there will be more exposure to diseases. Also since they have a little boy they will be very sensitive to any one coughing nearby. I imagine the first family carrying a bag full of medicine while the other taking none.

I mention this example to show that there are factors influencing the way you plan for your projects ( a trip is a project, isn't it ?). The two factors are:

- How sensitive you are to risks (Risk Tolerance). For a reason or another in some projects you will be willing to accept more risks and in other not. For example, you will be less tolerant to risks if you are on tight schedule.
- How much risks your project are exposed to. For example, a project in the time of global depression is unlike one in times of economic growth.

So, let's go back to this tool " Analytical techniques". There is no one technique to analyze something. It is just thinking deeply to understand your project and stakeholders.

*Note:* the term "Risk" is same as "Risk Exposure". They both referee to the formula of probability * impact

## 2 - Tools for Risk Identification

- **Documentation Review**

Reviewing documents will help you identify risks. You may search in documents such as plans for schedule, communication, quality, etc.

- **Information Gathering**

You can gather information by using a variety of techniques. PMBOK specifies the following methods:

- **Brainstorming**

This is a very effective tool for collecting as much information as possible. The brainstorming setup is very easy where people sit together and "think aloud" about a subject. You need a multidisciplinary team to get better ideas (ideas on risks of course). In addition, someone has to manage the session and encourage contributions (i.e. a facilitator). All ideas have to be recorded. Remember that, at this stage, it is not your goal to assess the validity of ideas.

- **Delphi Technique**

You will probably encounter many questions on the Delphi technique, so study this part carefully. Some key words indicating such in the exam are "expert consensus" and "anonymously". "Consensus" means "everyone agrees", "anonymously" means "without knowing who gave an opinion".

This technique is applied by having a facilitator who asks participants to give their opinions on a specific subject (this can be done via email). The facilitator will be the only one to know who gave an opinion and what the opinion was. Then the facilitator will share the results with participants and he/she will ask them for their opinions for the second time. Through many iterations of feedback, the facilitator's goal is for the whole body of participants, or the majority, to agree on one opinion.

- **Advantage:** Unlike brainstorming, participants are not under group pressure, since some people can be afraid of disagreeing with others or are too shy to express their opinions freely.
- **Disadvantage:** It is time consuming.

- **Example:** The project manager sends a separate email to seven stakeholders separately and asks them if the identified risk 'X' should be transferred to a third party to handle, thus increasing the cost of the project. He/she collects responses and omits the senders' names. Then he/she shares the responses with all participants hoping that they will align their opinions in a second run. He/she repeats this process until all or the majority of opinions are similarly aligned.

> The word Delphi is pronounced Del-fa-i. For your general information, the word refers to a place in old Greece where ancient people met with "wise people", who were called Oracles. Oracles answered the people's questions and predicted the future.

### ■ Interview

This tool is very effective in gathering information especially from experienced people (experts).

### ■ Root Cause Identification

Finding the root cause of a risk can be done by asking the question "what can cause the risk" two or three times. For the first time the question is asked, a cause should be identified. The second time the question is asked, a "cause of the first cause" should be identified. This process should be repeated until controlling the identified cause will truly prevent the risk from happening.

Root cause identification should be done in a meeting with individuals from the project team, stakeholders and experts, in order to improve the output through discussion and the sharing of expertise and knowledge.

The advantage of knowing the basic cause is that, although at the surface many risks will seem to be caused by different factors; in reality, many will share the same basic cause(s). By using root cause identification, you can control many risks with the same response; thus hitting several birds with one stone.

## ■ SWOT Analysis

This analysis will look at the project from different angles: strength, weakness, opportunity and threats (SWOT). SWOT analysis is useful for stimulating your thinking and will make you consider the positive risks as well.

Below is an example of a SWOT analysis on a tunnel digging project:

| Strength | Weakness | Opportunity | Threats |
|---|---|---|---|
| Largest machine in the world will be used for digging. | Staff are not familiar with the machine. | In some parts of the tunnel, the rock might be easier to dig into. | Underwater streams may be encountered. |

**Note:** The above example is simple and SWOT analyses can take many pages to complete.

## ■ Checklist Analysis

Your organization might use risks that were identified in previous projects to make a checklist of risks. A readymade list can also be used. The checklist helps to remind the project team of common and repeated risks in project management as well as of specific risks involving a particular type of project.

You should update the company's risk checklist with new risks identified from your project at the closeout phase.

## ■ Assumption Analysis

As discussed earlier, wrong assumptions are big sources of risks. In assumption analysis, you need to verify the rationality of the assumptions made. To analyze assumptions, you need them to be written out first. Analysis should be done by a team rather than having the project manager analyze the assumptions he/she has made.

## ■ Diagramming Techniques

Diagramming is simply to draw information visually to facilitate analysis. These techniques stimulate your thinking to find more and more risks.

# Inputs/Outputs

For the exam, you need to know the names of the diagramming techniques and what they are, but don't expect complex questions about them. The following are some of the diagramming techniques:

- **Ishikawa Diagram**

The Ishikawa diagram is also known as cause and effect or fishbone diagram. It is used in finding the causes of a problem (risks) by investigating how different factors can cause it. Usually, the factors assessed are: people, equipment, process and management (but you can use different factors as applicable). The fishbone diagram lets you systematically find the causes of a problem arising from different factors.

> **Note:**
> *This technique is often used in quality management, but can also be very helpful in risk management (so, for the exam, treat it as a risk management tool).*

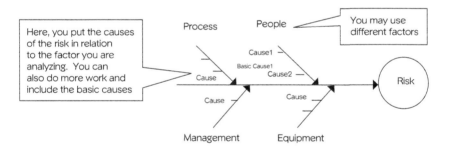

- **Process Flowcharts**

A flowchart is just a drawing of how a system operates. It helps you see the whole process and the links between its elements, thus making it easier to identify possible problems (risks).

- **Influence Diagram**

For the exam, just know that this is a technique for identifying risks involving how elements of a system can influence each other.

## 3 - Tools for Qualitative Risk Assessment

■ **Risk Matrix and Risk Assessment**

In practice, chances are that you will find many risks that may affect your project. During brainstorming, participants are encouraged to think of as many risks as they can. However, risks are not equal: some are more dangerous and complex, while some are hardly likely to occur, or are quite simple and easy to eliminate. Risk assessment is the tool that you use to prioritize the risks so that you would be able to develop a more efficient and effective risk response. Usually, you use a risk matrix to conduct risk assessment. The risk matrix is based on the risk formula: **Risk = Probability * Severity**

A simple risk matrix can look like the figure below:

The risk matrix is usually color coded where each cell has a color to indicate the level of risk (e.g. green for low risks, yellow for medium risks and red for high risks). For each possible risk, you should ask two questions:

First: What is the chance that the risk event will happen?
Second: If the risk event happens, what will be its effect on the project?

You can customize the risk matrix differently, for example you can substitute 'low', 'medium' and 'high' with numbers like '30%', '60%' and '100%'. You can also add more ranges like 'low', 'low to medium', 'medium to high' and 'high'. In addition, a company can have different matrices like, one for cost, schedule, quality, etc. The settings for probability and impact can be pre-defined. For example, a risk can be defined as low if it didn't happen in any previous similar project, and impact can be high if the cost impact is over a set monetary value (like $50,000).

> **Note:**
> Note: Most of the time, the word "risk" refers to negative outcomes, but it can also refer to positive outcomes. Positive risks are usually called opportunities, and, similar to negative risks, they depend on probability and impact (gains). The formula for opportunity can be written as:
>
> *Opportunity = Probability * Gain*

- **Assessment of the Quality of the Risk Data**

You need good ingredients for a good output. Data quality assessment is concerned with how confident you are about the risk facts (i.e. how they were identified and are they fully understood). Consider the example of risk identification or prioritization that was done by a single person. The quality of the output might not be as good as that which was studied and formulated by a multidisciplinary and experienced team.

- **Risk Categorization**

In risk categorization, you group risks under common sources (categories). For example, you can group risks related to governmental authorities and suppliers under the category "External Risks". Risk categorization is based on the Risk Breakdown Structure (RBS), which looks similar to the WBS. You can make an RBS for your project, or find a general one that is adopted by the organization.

> **Risk categorization can help you in two areas:**
>
> Risk Identification, Because you can use the RBS as a checklist to make sure that you have systematically gone over all the possible sources of risks.
>
> Risk Response, When similar risks are grouped together, you may be able to identify common responses to them.
>
> **Note:** Expect some questions about RBS. Remember, it is used to represent categories of risks. Do not confuse RBS with WBS!

The following is an example of an RBS:

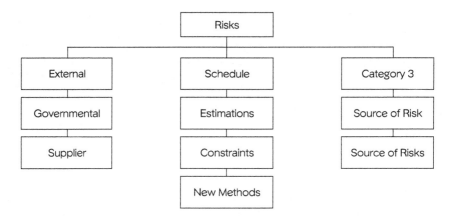

## Risk Urgency Assessment

This is another way of prioritizing risks (remember, prioritizing risks is THE purpose of risk assessment). Here, you will rank risks based on how urgent they are. If you believe that a risk will happen early on in your project, you have to give it more weight.

> *Note:* There are different dimensions that you may use to assess risks, such as probability, severity and urgency. They are all indicators of the magnitude of risks. However, risk urgency might not be as strong an indicator as probability and severity are.

## 4 - Tools for Quantitative Risk Analysis

### Interviews and Expert Judgment

You already know that interviews can be used as a tool in risk identification. You can also use them in risk assessment. Here you sit with experienced people and ask them to provide estimations on probability and severity for risks.

- *Example*:

You need to know how long it will take to design a web interface for a database. To do that, you arrange an interview with an expert (like the senior system analyst, for example) and he/she tells you it should take about 80 hours, but not more than 100 hours in the worst case and not less than 70 hours if everything goes well. In turn, you can use these numbers in the three-point estimation formula to find a more reliable expected value.

> **Note:** You need high quality data, so during the interview make sure to ask the expert on what basis he/she established the said estimation.

> **Note:** As a project manager, you need to identify and invite experts who are relevant to your project, but be aware of their bias. Bias is the attitude of favoring a certain outcome without thoroughly considering other outcomes. For example, an expert would recommend Technique_1 over Technique_2 simply because he/she is more familiar with the former technique than the latter. Many factors can affect a person's judgment, such as experience and personal interest. A good way of dealing with bias is to ask the expert to explain why he/she is giving a particular response.

- **Sensitivity Analysis**

This technique is adopted to identify the risks that have the strongest effect on a project. Sensitivity analysis is usually represented by a tornado diagram (refer to the Math Section in Chapter 2).

- **Expected Monetary Value and Decision Tree Analysis**

These techniques were discussed in the Math Section of Chapter 2. They provide you with the anticipated cost(s) of risks. Once you know how much each risk may cost, you will be able to compare and rank them. For example, a risk that will cost you a loss of $10,000 is in greater need of an elaborate response than one costing you $1,500.

# Chapter 5

## ■ Simulation

You use simulation to evaluate the effect of risks on the project as a whole. In simulation, you use mathematical calculations and computers to predict how your project will perform. Based on the simulation result(s), you might find that your budget and/or timeframe are not realistic, giving you an opportunity to amend them before embarking on the project.

> *Note:* You apply simulation to your project with the identified risks before you make a plan to respond to them. After making a response plan, incorporate your responses in the simulation model and run it again to see if the result improves (which indicates a good response plan).

### • *Example:*

After you have identified the risks and included them in your simulation, you found that your project might undergo a 30-day delay. Therefore, you designed different strategies to respond to the identified risks. These responses would decrease the magnitude of the risks, and when you re-simulate you would get a delay result of only 5 days, for example.

## 5 - Tools for Risk Response

### • Strategies for Threat and Opportunity

Risks can be either good or bad. Positive risks are called opportunities; negative risks are called threats (or just risks). Tools here are the strategies (options) that you select to control risks.

The table below summarizes the strategies you can take (try to figure out what they are, based on their names).

| Threat | Opportunity | When to Use it |
|---|---|---|
| Avoid | Exploit | For risks that are too good to miss or too bad to let happen |
| Transfer | Share | For risks (good or bad) you cannot deal with by yourself and need the help of another party |
| Mitigate | Enhance | You balance between risks and resources. You work on the components of risks (probability and impact) to reduce threats and improve opportunity AS MUCH AS YOU CAN |
| Accept | Accept | This is for risks that you cannot control through any of the above strategies. If they happen, they happen. However, you can put some money aside to deal with them (called contingency reserve) |

- It is better to use a mix of strategies.
- You can use decision trees to choose between strategies.
- You cannot always just choose any strategy you want. There will be risks that you will not be able to avoid or transfer.
- You can identify primary and secondary strategies. For example, you plan to avoid a risk, but after initial failure, you try to mitigate it.
- Risk response will require some change(s) in the project plan (resources, time, quality, contract terms, etc.).
- If you accept a risk, you usually have to allocate a budget to deal with it if it occurs. That budget is referred to as contingency reserve.

The following is detailed description of each strategy:

## **Strategies for Threats**

- **Avoid**

Avoiding a risk means that you do not want it to happen, ever, and, hence, you try to eliminate it. You will be willing to invest resources or change your project plan to do that. A simple example is a project for a vacation in Europe. In one of your destinations, you were only able to find a flight schedule that will make you miss other flights that are essential in your trip project. You avoid this risk by simply eliminating that destination. Another example is that of a project involving the manufacture of a sports car with very wide fenders. You realize that these fenders will pose a high risk of limiting the angle of door opening, thus making it difficult to enter the car. You are unable to reduce the risk and will then decide simply to remove the wide fenders from the design.

> *Note:* In many cases, avoiding risks will mean that you change your project plan and lose some benefits. In the two examples above, you will lose a trip to one place in Europe, and will lose the look and appeal of having wide fenders in the car.

- **Transfer**

Transfer is a strategy that usually applies to threats that you do not have any experience dealing with. You may also apply this strategy if you find it more practical to let others handle some of the project risks.

- *Example:*

You need to get approval from a governmental environment authority before you start constructing a tower. To avoid the risk of delay, you hire a specialist legal office to follow up on the matter.

The option of responding to risks via "transfer" is a key reason why you should do risk management before project procurement, as you may need to include risk transfer arrangements in the contracts.

- **Mitigate**

This strategy applies to risks that you cannot avoid or transfer. It is like doing the best you can with the available resources to reduce the risks (by reducing their probability or severity or both).

- *Example:*

During the foundation work for a building, you needed a pump to work continuously for a long period of time. There is a risk of work delay if the pump fails. Here, you can mitigate the threats of pump failure by installing another parallel pump, thus reducing the load on the first one and the probability of failure.

## Strategies for Opportunities

- **Exploit**

Here, you don't want to lose an expected opportunity. You try to manage your resources so that the opportunity will not be wasted. You can think of it as the opposite of avoiding a risk.

- *Example:*

If you finish Task X one day ahead of schedule, then you can combine resources for Task Y and save money. The project manager in this situation may increase shift time for Task X or put more experienced staff to work on that task, in order to ensure that it will be completed one day earlier.

- **Share**

In your project, you can have an opportunity but do not have the expertise or resources to benefit from it. In this case, it is better to share some of the benefits with someone who can actually make it happen than lose it all.

- *Example:*

In a project to dig for oil, you sign a contract with a gas company to capture any natural gas that might be discovered and share the profits.

- **Enhance**

Similar in concept to mitigation, you want to improve chances of an opportunity by increasing its probability or positive impact.

*Example:*

There is a chance that equipment X will be available before the planned schedule, thus enabling an early start. To enhance this, you assign a member of the project team to establish close contact with the equipment supplier to improve the chance of early delivery.

## Strategy for Both Threats and Opportunities

- **Accept**

If there is no suitable strategy for dealing with threats or opportunities, then you may choose to accept them. All strategies mentioned so far will involve some modification in the project plan, but if you accept a risk, you just let it happen (if it happens at all; remember that risks are in the future and they may or may not happen).

*There are two types of acceptance:*

- Passive Acceptance: You do nothing regarding the risk; for example, if an equipment delivery is delayed, you just wait.
- Active Acceptance: You assign extra money, time, resources aside, in order to deal with the risks. This is called a contingency reserve; for example, if an equipment delivery is delayed, you rent one to perform the task.

> **Note:** *If you accept a risk, even with a contingency reserve, you will act only if the risk happens (during project execution). In other strategies, you will act before the risk happens (during project planning).*

> **Note:** *There is another type of reserve called management reserve. PMBOK describes the management reserve as:*
>
> - *It is money set aside for unplanned and unidentified changes to the project.*
> - *The project manager might need approval to use it.*
> - *This reserve is not part of the cost baseline.*

The management reserve is usually predetermined in companies. For example, it may be 2.5% of the budget for each project. As for the contingency reserve, it is identified based on calculations and reasoning.

- *Example:*

You planned a visit to Thailand and put a budget to cover your transportation, accommodation and entertainment (this is your budget). Then you thought of the risk of bad weather delaying your flight back home (which you can do nothing about) and, so, you allocated extra money to spend in case you have to stay in a hotel (this is your contingency reserve). Now, what about risks that you can't anticipate; such as falling sick and needing medical care? For these "miscellaneous" risks, you set yet an extra sum of money (this is your management reserve). So you have the cost of the vacation + the contingency reserve + the management reserve.

■ General Example

Consider the risk of an equipment delay; let us see how you can select different strategies to manage it. Your selection of the strategy will depend on factors like the importance of the equipment, availability of different suppliers and the risk tolerance of stakeholders.

| Strategy | Your Goal | What You Might Do |
| --- | --- | --- |
| Avoid | Equipment MUST arrive | If possible, do the work with other equipment that is available (substitute). Alternatively, if possible, eliminate the activity that requires the use of the equipment |
| Mitigate | Ensure as much as possible, that the equipment arrives on time | Reduce the chance of delay by establishing close contacts with the supplier. You may also look for other suppliers who, you believe, are more reliable |
| Transfer | Make it the problem of another party | If possible, make a third party handle the work that requires the use of the equipment |
| Accept | You can do nothing to prevent the delay | Either wait for delivery or assign money to rent a replacement |

### ■ Contingency Planning

Contingency planning is a risk response tool that is used when the risk actually happens. It involves monitoring triggers. Triggers are early indicators that a risk is going to happen.

. *Example:*

You identified a risk of increase in diesel prices and made a contingency plan to fill up all your storage tanks. Your triggers will be diesel prices and you should keep monitoring them until they reach a pre-defined level which will be the time to execute your plan. Another example is a contingency plan to utilize more programmers if your software project falls behind schedule. Your trigger here might be missing a milestone.

Personally, I think of contingency plans as something like an emergency evacuation of a building on fire. You make the plan and keep it until you see triggers like smoke or hear the fire alarm.

> **Note:** Do not confuse the contingency reserve with contingency planning. The former is done if you accept a risk and allocate some money (or time) to deal with risks. The latter is a plan that you execute if the trigger(s) happen.

- **Expert Judgment**

This is another tool that is used in risk response. You might consult an expert to advise you on how to deal with risks and control them. Using experts is justified because they have a better understanding of risks in their field of expertise. Note that you use the judgments of experts at different times, when identifying risks, analyzing risks and responding to risks.

## 6 - Tools for Risk Monitoring and Control

During project execution, there should be performance reports to inform the project manager on how the project is progressing. If you notice that your project is not performing well, it may be due to new risks or risks that were identified but not properly controlled.

- **Risk Reassessment**

Risk reassessment will be done during the project's execution phase for existing risks plus any new ones. Risk reassessment should be done at predefined dates (or in the periodic project meetings). However, if you notice that new risks are happening at an alarming rate, you should call for specific meeting(s) on risk reassessment.

> **Note:** Read the exam questions carefully (do not confuse reassessment with assessment). During reassessment, you can use the same tools done in risk assessment.

- **Status Meetings**

In these meetings, you will discuss with your team and the stakeholders how your project is progressing compared to your initial plan (baseline). During these meetings, you should put risk management on the agenda for an opportunity to discuss various aspects of risks in the project.

- **Risk Audits**

To conduct an audit means to examine and verify. By performing an audit, you can show how effective your risk management activities are/were. Your goal is to verify that the risk identification, assessment and response activities done during the planning phase were adequate. Note that you need to document your audit findings and may use a special template for them. You may also invite some stakeholders to participate in the audits.

- **Reserve Analysis**

Do you remember the contingency reserve you used when you decided to accept risks? Here, you will simply investigate how much has remained and whether it will be enough to cover the remaining risks. This will help you to decide whether you need to request more money for the reserve or release some of the reserve as needed. For example, if you utilized 80% of the reserve and only half of the risks that need the reserve happened, then you might anticipate cost overrun and prepare yourself and the project by asking for more money from the project sponsor(s).

- **Performance Measurement**

If actual performance is poor compared to the planned performance, you should check for new risks or re-examine previously identified risks.

- **Variance and Trend Analysis**

Variance and trend analysis are monitoring and forecasting methods used to monitor project performance. They utilize techniques like the earned value analysis to predict future performance based on past and current one(s). For example, if the S-curve shows that you will exceed the budget, then you should investigate the reasons and risks that caused the deviation from the baseline.

# Inputs

## Inputs for Risk Management

Below is a description of all inputs you will use in risk management. Familiarize yourself with the inputs below and make sure that you understand what they represent and in which risk processes they are used.

- **Activity Cost Estimation / Activity Duration Estimation**

Risks may be found in time and cost estimations. You can review your estimates and validate the assumptions on which the estimates were done. You can also check if the experts who helped in the estimates were biased. An example of validation is to verify if a technician's hourly rate, which was used in the calculations of the cost plan, is correct.

- **Stakeholder Register**

The stakeholder register is used as an input in risk identification. You need the register in order to know the contact information of the stakeholders so that you could invite them to participate in risk identification activities such as brainstorming sessions. In addition, you will find stakeholders expectations in the register and you should review them for possible conflicts with the project scope (and with each other). You need to make sure that the register includes all the relevant stakeholders.

- **Cost/Schedule/Quality Management Plans**

You need these documents because they will help you identify risks during the risk identification process. You will find information, like quality requirements, which will help you determine possible risks in achieving them. In addition, these plans will enable you to know about the methods that are used for preparing the cost/time estimates and for identifying possible inconsistencies and conflicts.

> *Note:* As you can see from this input, risk management requires you to review different plans for your project to identify inconsistencies, mistakes and conflicts. I take this chance to support my earlier statement that risk management helps bring everything together in your project.

- **Scope Statement/Scope Baseline**

Scope Statement: If you want to "get to know" the project, you need to refer to the scope statement. It spells out what will be included in the project and what will not be. It contains useful information for risk management; like deliverables, constraints and assumptions.

***Scope Baseline:*** It is basically the scope statement plus the work breakdown structure.

You need to know about the scope, because it will tell you how large and complex your project is. This information will help you to decide on how elaborate your risk management activities should be. For example, large and complex projects might need risk simulation, unlike small projects.

In addition, you will use the scope baseline to identify risks, because it contains information such as the assumption log, constraints and the WBS. You need to examine assumptions and validate them as they can lead to unanticipated risks. The WBS will help you to see the project with its different tasks in a holistic manner.

- **Project Documentation**

PMBOK uses the term project documents to refer to supporting documents that are not included in your project plan. Your project plan will include sections for the nine knowledge areas plus the scope, cost and schedule baseline. Project documents contain other information such as registers (including the risk register), logs, metrics, and work method statements. If you want to read more on project documentation, refer to PMBOK 4th edition, Appendix A.

- **Enterprise Environmental Factors**

Imagine that you are writing an article describing your company in a business magazine. What information will you include? How about:

- Company's vision and mission
- Company's organizational structure (is it functional, matrix or projectized)
- Culture: shared value, worker behavior, blame culture, behavior in meetings… etc
- Marketplace
- Regulatory standards

The list above is an example of what is included in the Enterprise Environmental Factors. Don't expect to find a folder named Enterprise Environmental Factors, but rather information will be scattered in the organization and some of which might be observed rather than documented.

*Risk tolerance* is part of the environmental factors and it tells you how sensitive people are to risks. High tolerance means having "more space" to deal with risks and vice versa. For example, if you are managing a project that is not essential for your company's strategic plan, then there might be more tolerance toward risks (i.e. more relaxed reaction if the project is facing difficulties). Higher tolerance also implies that stakeholders (specifically the sponsor) are less willing to spend a lot of money to control risks. The key here is to know how your project relates to what matters most for the stakeholders.

- **Organizational Process Assets**

These are documented "ways of doing business". They might include policies and standards to be followed in risk management; like an official risk matrix and risk templates. In addition, they include lessons learnt. The custodians of these documents will vary from one company to another. For example, you might find the approved risk matrix in the quality and risk department and the lessons learnt in a database run by a knowledge management office.

- **Communication Management Plan**

The communication management plan is helpful in risk planning. You may use it to identify and invite stakeholders for brainstorming sessions on risk identification.

- **Performance Reports**

Information about project performance will help you to check how risks actually affect your project, and identify trends.


- **Project charter:** project charter is the "go-ahead" document. It signals the official start of the project, signed by senior managers and have general information about objectives, duration and the budget. The project manager is usually named in the charter and major risks are identified.

- **Procurement documents:** for example request for quotation and request for proposal (RFP). These documents are important for risk management because they need to accurately describe the service or product the project want to buy. Such accuracy is not always easy especially for new products. In addition, make sure to follow the company procedures for issuing such documents.

- **Human resource management plan:** you will develop an HR plan for your project. It will contain the organization structure for your project plus roles and responsibly. In addition, you will find the total number of staff needed and from where you will get them.

# Outputs

In the different risk management processes, you will have the following outputs:

- **Contract Agreement Updates**

During risk response, you may identify response strategies like risk transfer and sharing. Your contract agreement must be updated to reflect how risks will be distributed between the client and the contractors.

- **Updated Organizational Process Assets**

You used the organizational process assets as an input to find information such as the lessons learnt and the templates on risk management (like the risk matrix). It is possible that, during the project, you have identified the need to modify templates and to add new lessons learnt. New additions should be documented in order to benefit future projects.

- **Change Requests**

After conducting risk responses, you should have most of the project risks under control before you start execution. By "under control", I mean that you have identified proper responses and integrated them in your project plan. However, during execution, you might face new risks and events that might prompt you to implement a contingency plan. To deal with these risks, you usually need to change your project plan through a change request. Change requests can include:

- **Preventive Actions:** Example: you identified new risks during risk reassessment and want to decrease their chance of occurrence or impact (here the risk has not occurred yet).

- **Corrective Actions:** These are actions done to deal with risks that already occurred, like those which deal with unidentified risks (workarounds); or risks that have contingency plans prepared for them. Implementing workarounds or contingency plans involves changes to the project plan.
- **Workarounds:** Are responses to unplanned risks that occur during project execution. I like to think about the concept of workarounds with the following example. Imagine that while you are driving in a forested area, a deer jumps into the road. You take an immediate decision of driving around it and, hopefully, saving the deer's life and yours.

An example from project management on workarounds can be an unexpected "new crane" failure in a construction project. The project manager can work around this event by renting another crane. Note that renting another crane will cost money but it should be less than the cost of project delay until the original crane is fixed. In addition, the project manager will need to submit a change request for the rented crane as this will change your cost plan by the amount of the rental fee.

- **Project Document Updates**

As you progress through risk management activities, you will have new information available. You need to update existing documents like technical method statements. For example: after risk response, you decide to do one task in a different way using new technology in order to minimize risk. Therefore, the work method statement must be updated to reflect the usage of the new technology.

## Inputs and Outputs

Some of the outputs in the risk management process are used as inputs in other processes. For example, you will see the risk register as an input and as an output in most processes.

## Risk Management Plan

The risk management plan will be the first thing you produce in risk management. It will be developed (i.e. an output) in the first risk management process and then used as input in most of the remaining processes. It is very important since it contains the following information:

### 1- Methodology

As you know, every project is unique and will demand a unique approach for risk management. Here, you will specify how risk planning will be conducted. You may, for example, pick brainstorming and the Delphi technique for risk identification in your project.

### 2 - Definition of Probability and Impact

The risk plan has to establish a common understanding of probability and impact scores. For example, when a stakeholder says that the probability is high, it should roughly mean the same thing to all other stakeholders. The risk management plan should contain guidelines on how to measure probability and impact. Consider the following example of guidelines on how to score impacts:

| Impact (Score) | When |
| --- | --- |
| Low | Less than 5% increase in project duration |
| Medium | More than 8% increase in project duration |
| High | More than 12% increase in project duration |

- Notice that the scoring above is based on project duration. You can specify impact on other parameters such as scope and/or cost.
- You can also specify when probability is low, medium or high. For example, probability can be high if the event has happened repeatedly in past projects.
- You can have more levels on your scale ( like: very low, low, medium, high, very high)
- You can use numbers instead of words (like low = 30%, medium 60% and high = 90%)

- Although not very common, the impact scale can be nonlinear. A nonlinear scale is a non-proportional scale that is used to maximize or minimize certain events by giving more/less weight to them. For example, you can define scores as follows:
low = 0.2, medium = 0.7 and high = 0.9
Note that this type of scoring gives more weight to medium and high levels of risk than to low levels of risks. It might be because stakeholders have low risk tolerance.

Remember that probability and impact are defined and scored differently between industries, companies and projects. By setting guidelines, we do not want to rule out the importance of experience and good judgment, but rather we attempt to establish a reference to control the subjectivity of the scoring.

### 3 - Risk Matrix

Different companies will have customized risk matrices, so make sure to use the official one in your project.

### 4 - Stakeholders Tolerance

You should include information about risk tolerance in the risk management plan. Knowing how tolerant your stakeholders are to risk will help you make better decisions. Example: there is conflict in scoring the impact of a risk as either low or medium. If you know that the tolerance is high, then you may select the low score. Risk tolerance is not something that you will find in the company's annual report. You will need to do some research about the company and you will need to interview the stakeholders. You will also need to study the scope of the project and the way it affects the organizational objectives. Keep in mind that tolerance can change from one project to another.

### 5 - Risk Category

Remember that the purpose of the risk management plan is to guide you on how to go about risk management. Risk categories will help you systematically to identify risks during the risk identification process and, hence, they are included in this plan.

### 6 - Roles and Responsibilities

In this section of the risk plan, you will specify who will do what in the risk management process, e.g. who will be involved in risk identification and who will call for meetings (don't confuse this with the roles and responsibilities assigned to risk owners during risk response planning).

### 7 - Budgeting

Under this heading of the risk management plan, you should include what resources are needed to conduct risk management (like meeting rooms, multimedia equipment, risk simulation software, etc.) and how much risk management activities are expected to cost the project.

### 8 - Timing

How long your risk management activities will take. For example, you may schedule two days for risk identification.

### 9 - Reporting Format

Under this section, you may say, for example, that risks will be documented in the risk register and will be communicated as per the communication plan. You may also include a template for the risk register.

### 10 - Tracking

How do you record and audit risk management activities? You can create a folder to collect all information about risk management like minutes of meetings and the risk register. It is then possible to audit the folder for completeness and use it to identify lessons learnt.

> **Note:** The risk management plan contains much valuable information. To help you remember its contents, think of them as tools that will help you implement and organize your risk management activities.

## Project Management Plan

This is the "mother of all plans" which is created at the end of the project planning phase and has all the information needed to start executing and monitoring your project. Think of it as a big folder with sections that include plans for scope, schedule, cost, quality, HR management, communication, risk and procurement. In the course of the risk management activities, you will use/update your project plan as follows:

***During Risk Response (Output):*** Here you need to update the project plan based on your risk response. For example: In order to avoid a risk of delay in a certain task, you decided to add an additional programmer to your IT project team. This will cost you more and that must be reflected in the project plan (cost section).

***During Risk Control (As an Input):*** At this time, your project is in execution phase and you need the project management plan because it contains the risk management plan. You need it to follow on the implementation of risk control.

***During Risk Control (As an Output):*** In risk monitoring, there are usually change requests that are made. The relevant section of the project plan should be revised to highlight the changes. Example: A change request to move a task backward in the project timeline will be reflected in an updated schedule. Can you think of other changes that can affect cost, quality and scope?

> ***Note:*** *Be comfortable that the project plan is a collection of many plans. Some people think of it as only the schedule or Gantt chart, but it is much more than that. In essence, you use the project plan in all the risk processes because you always need some of its sections for future reference.*

## Risk Register

*Register: A written list (record)*

Consider the risk register as the most important input/output in risk management. A risk register is a document that contains risks, their rank, response strategies, etc. The risk register is created during the risk identification phase and is updated throughout the remaining risk processes until project closeout. To help you remember the content of the risk register in each process, I advise you to think of the tools that you use and what the outcome of using each tool can be.

## 1- Risk Register in Risk Identification

- **As an Output**

You have identified the risks and need a place to log them. Most likely, you will be using a template that is customized to your project or company, but whatever template you will use, it must contain a column for risks. The risk register will include, at this stage:

*Main Output*

- List of Identified Risks

*Other Outputs*

In addition to the list of risks, you may be able to find the following:

- Root Causes of Risks
- Potential Responses

If you are able to guess a risk's root causes or potential responses, you should log them in the register and validate them in later stages.

## 2- Risk Register during Qualitative Risk Analysis

Your goal here is to arrange the identified risks in a way that helps you to have a more effective risk response.

- **As an Input**

You need the risk register because it contains the list of identified risks that you need to prioritize.

- **As an Output, The Risk Register Will Contain:**

*Main Output*

During risk qualitative analysis, you use tools to prioritize risks. Thus, your main output is the prioritization of the already identified risks. You can prioritize risks in different ways, such as by grouping them in categories like high, medium and low, or by numbering them sequentially.

*Other Outputs*

These outputs are derived from the main output stated above. They are generated through deeper analysis, arrangement and by making different representations of the prioritized risks:

**Watch List:** The risks that were ranked with low effect on the project can be excluded from further analysis and response, but you still need to keep an eye on them, hence, you should group them in the "watch list" and then attach the said list to the risk register. Consider the watch list as a first filter to reduce the number of risks to which you will apply responses.

Note that stakeholders' risk tolerance will play an important role in determining how big your watch list is. If the tolerance is low, you will have a smaller list because you will need to respond to more risks and control them.

**Urgent Risks:** A tool that you use in qualitative assessment is urgency assessment. Here you have to come up with a list of risks that require immediate response(s). Arranging risks by their level of urgency can help you to organize your risk response(s) in a better way.

**Categories of Risks:** Another tool you use in qualitative assessment is risk categorization. If you know the risk category, then you may design better response(s) to them. Some risks will share the same sources and you may be able to control them by using the same response.

**Other Representations:** These can facilitate and improve risk response, e.g. noting trends and areas that need more attention.

## 3- Risk Register during Quantitative Risk Analysis

In this process, your goal is to test the effect of the risks "virtually, via modeling and simulation" on your project.

- **As an Input**

You need the register for the list of the prioritized risks. Quantitative analysis is more expensive than qualitative analysis, and it is a good way to focus on a selected number of risks.

- **As an Output, the Risk Register Will Contain:**

List of Prioritized Risks: Now, your list of risks is more objective and you know with more confidence which risk has a bigger impact on your project. This updated risk prioritization should help you to undertake better response actions by utilizing more of your resources on more important risks.

Probability Analysis of the Project: You will have information on the probability of achieving your objectives. For example, after simulation you may find that the probability of finishing the project on time is 70%.

## 4- The Risk Register during Risk Response

Your goal now is to address all the risks and control as many of them as possible.

- **As an Input**

You need the risk register for the list of prioritized risks.

- **As an Output, the Risk Register Will Contain:**

*Main Output*

- List of Responses for Each Risk
- Roles and Responsibilities: For each risk, you will identify who is responsible for implementing the corresponding response. Sometimes, different parties will need to work together to achieve a response, but there must be one clearly accountable person. In addition, you may assign responders from outside the project. However, this must be clearly communicated to them and you must secure their commitment.

*Other Outputs*

- Contingency Plans and Events that Trigger their Use
- Contingency Reserve
- Fallback Plans: You may set up a backup plan if your initial response fails (Plan B). For Example: In your IT project, you plan to negotiate with the IT manager to secure additional programmers, however, if you fail, you will have to hire them on short-term contracts.
- Residual Risks: Risks that remain after implementing the risk response (because it might not have been practical to respond to each and every individual risk).
- Accepted Risks: Risks that you did not design a response strategy for them.
- Secondary Risks: Risks that result from implementing the risk response (you may call it the by-product of risk response). For example, increasing work shifts to reduce delays in accomplishing a task may produce another risk of lower quality output due to workers' fatigue.

## 5- The Risk Register during Risk Monitoring and Control

### ■ As an Input

You need the register because it contains all the information about risks, such as the complete list of risks, responses, who is responsible for implementing the responses, watch list, fallback plans, contingency plans, etc.

### ■ As an InputAs an Output, the Risk Register will contain:

**New Risks:** Risks that were identified during the execution stage. This will also include their analysis and response.

**Outcome of Risk Response:** You should record the actual outcome of each response so you would be able to compare it to what was expected. In addition, you should include (or attach) the result of your risk audits.

> See how we have built on the risk register to make it grow little by little?

# Chapter 6:
# Exercises to Remember Inputs, Outputs and Tools

Chapter 6

# Exercises to Remember Inputs, Outputs and Tools

In the previous chapter, you were introduced to the different components of the risk management processes. Now, it is time to master the location of each component.

For each process, you will find a figure with all the inputs, tools and outputs that you need to remember. Immediately after, you will find the same figure (but empty) for you to fill. After you go through all the six processes, you will find that the exercise is repeated, to improve information retention.

> **Note:** It might be helpful to remember the count of the components for each process. For example, if you know that there are four inputs for quantitative analysis, then you can check if you are missing some. In addition, I follow a certain sequence for drawing each process, as follows:
>
> First, I identify the tools. Then, I think of what they can produce, and hence figure out the output. In the end, I think of the outputs and from where they may be derived and thus fill in the inputs.

As this is a multiple choice exam, you don't need to remember the exact wording for each component as long as you know what each means. For example, in PMBOK there is a tool in qualitative assessment called "Risk Data Quality Assessment", I find the name confusing and just call it quality of risk data (or quality of risk information).

> **Note:** This exercise is based on the most important figure to remember for the exam, which is The Project Risk Management Overview (reproduced by permission from the Project Management Institute- A Guide to the Project Management Body of Knowledge (PMBOK® Guide) - Fifth Edition, Project Management Institute, Inc., 2013.)

# Exercises to Remember Inputs, Outputs and Tools

## Project Risk Management Overview

### 11.1 Plan Risk Management

1 - Inputs
 1 - Project management plan
 2 - Project charter
 3 - Stakeholder register
 4 - Enterprise environmental factors
 5 - Organizational process assets

2 - Tools & Techniques
 1 - Analytical techniques
 2 - Expert judgment
 3 - Meetings

3 - Outputs
 1 - Risk management plan

### 11.2 Identify Risks

1 - Inputs
 1 - Risk management plan
 2 - Cost management plan
 3 - Schedule management plan
 4 - Quality management plan
 5 - Human resource management plan
 6 - Scope baseline
 7 - Activity cost estimates
 8 - Activity duration estimates
 9 - Stakeholder register
 10 - Project documents
 11 Procurement documents
 12 - Enterprise environmental factors
 13 - Organizational Process assets

2 - Tools & Techniques
 1 - Documentation Reviews
 2 - Information gathering techniques
 3 - Checklist analysis
 4 - Assumptions analysis
 5 - Diagramming techniques
 6 - SWOT analysis
 7 - Expert judgment

3 - Outputs
 1 - Risk register

### 11.3 Perform Qualitative Risk Analysis

1 - Inputs
 1 - Risk management plan
 2 - Scope baseline
 3 - Risk Register
 4 - Enterprise enironmental factors
 5 - Organizational process assets

2 - Tools & Techniques
 1 - Risk probability and impact assessment
 2 - Probability and impact matrix
 3 - Risk data quality assessment
 4 - Risk categorization
 5 - Risk urgency assessment
 6 - Expert judgment

3 - Outputs
 1 - project documents updates

### 11.4 Perform Quantitative Risk Analysis

1 - Inputs
 1 - Risk management plan
 2 - Cost management plan
 3 - Schedule management plan
 4 - Risk register
 5 - Enterprise environmental factors
 6 - Organizational process assets

2 - Tools & Techniques
 1 - Date gathering and representation techniques
 2 - Quantitative risk analysis and modeling techniques
 3 - Expert judgment

3 - Outputs
 1 - project documents updates

### 11.5 Plan Risk Responses

1 - Inputs
 1 - Risk management plan
 2 - Risk register

2 - Tools & Techniques
 1 - Strategies for negative risks or threats
 2 - Strategies for positive risks or opportunities
 3 - Contingent response strategies
 4 - Expert judgment

3 - Outputs
 1 - Project management plan updates
 2 - Project documents updates

### 11.6 Control Risks

1 - Inputs
 1 - Project managemnt plan
 2 - Risk register
 3 - Work performance data
 4 - Work performance reports

2 - Tools & Techniques
 1 - Risk reassessment
 2 - Risk audits
 3 - Variance and trend analysis
 4 - Technical performance measurement
 5 - Reserve analysis
 6 - Meetings

3 - Outputs
 1 - Work performance information
 2 - Change requests
 3 - Project management plan updates
 4 - Project documents updates
 5 - Organizational process assets updates

**Project Risk Management Overview (PMBOK, 5th Edition)**

# Chapter 6

## Exercise 1

### Risk Planning Process

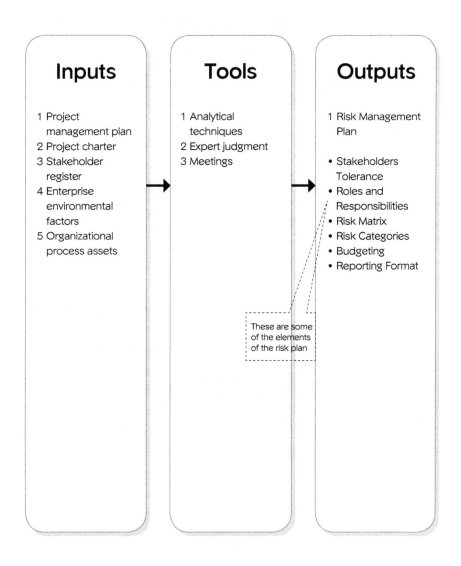

**Exercises to Remember Inputs, Outputs and Tools**

Fill in the Blanks

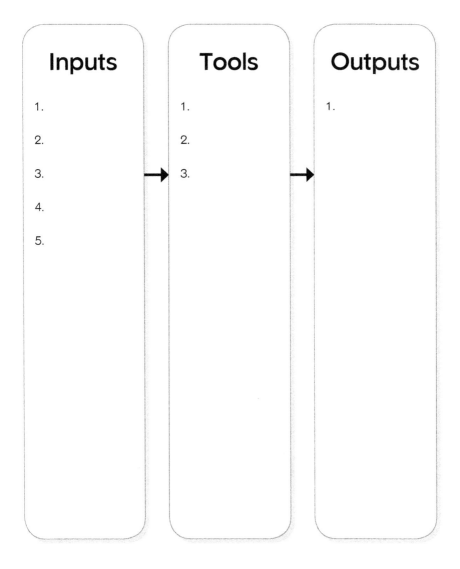

101

Chapter 6

## Risk Identification Process

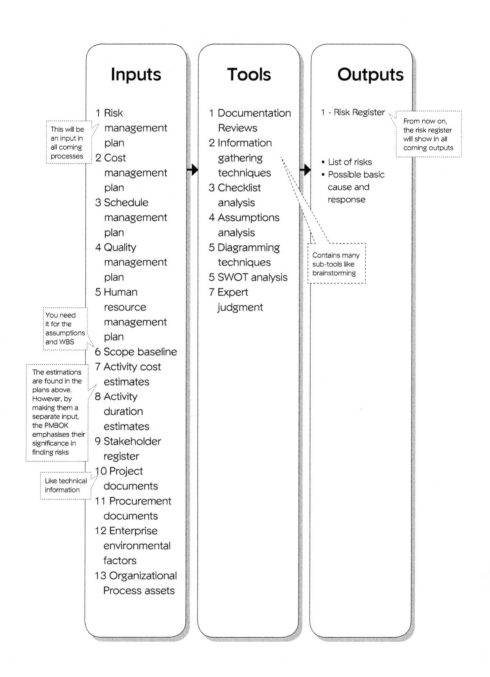

# Exercises to Remember Inputs, Outputs and Tools

Fill in the Blanks

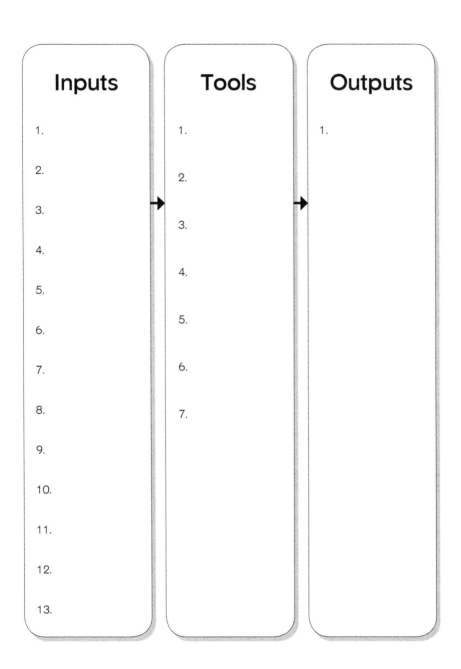

## Risk Qualitative Analysis Process

### Inputs

1. Risk management plan
2. Scope baseline
3. Risk Register
4. Enterprise enironmental factors
5. Organizational process assets

### Tools

1. Risk probability and impact assessment
2. Probability and impact matrix
3. Risk data quality assessment
4. Risk categorization
5. Risk urgency assessment
6. Expert judgment

### Outputs

1 - Risk Register Updates

- List of prioritized risks
- Watch List
- Risk Categories
- Urgent Risks

**Exercises to Remember Inputs Outputs and Tools**

Fill in the Blanks

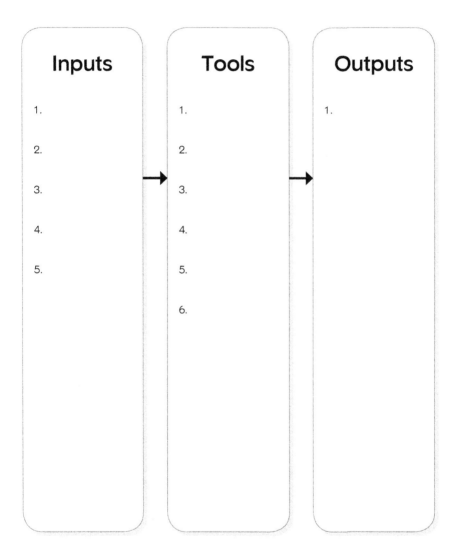

# Chapter 6

## Risk Quantitative Analysis Process

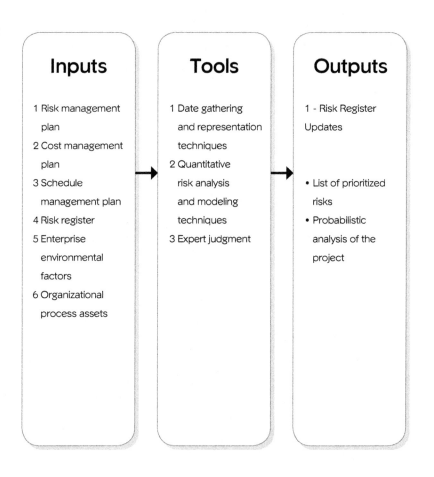

# Exercises to Remember Inputs, Outputs and Tools

Fill in the Blanks

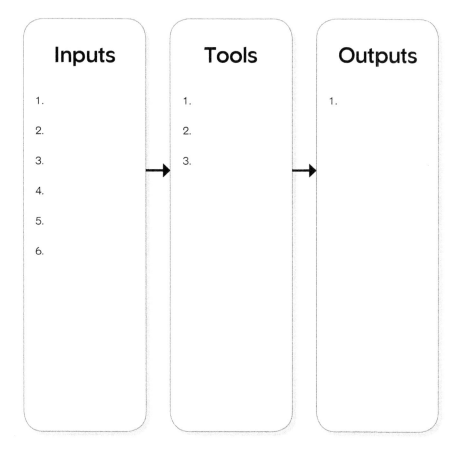

# Chapter 6

## Risk Response Planning Process

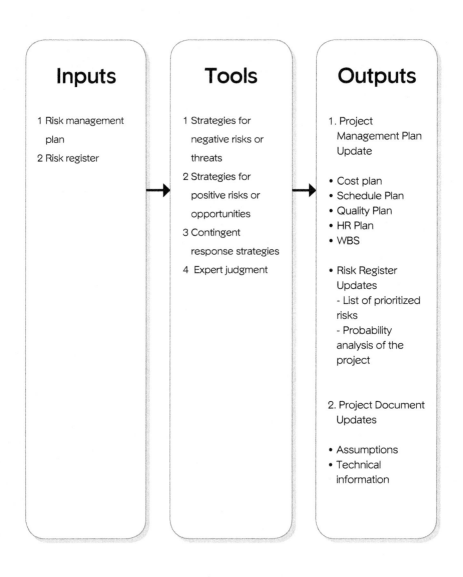

# Exercises to Remember Inputs, Outputs and Tools

Fill in the Blanks

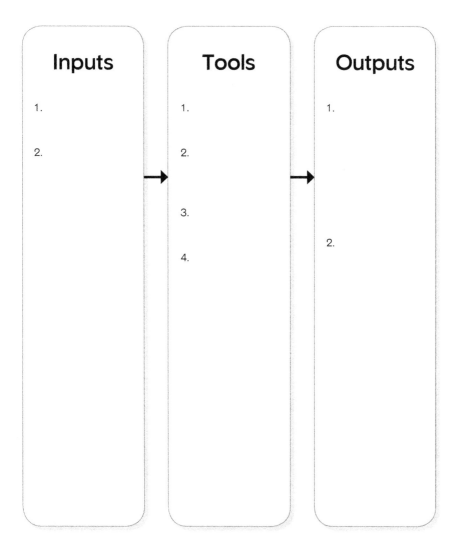

# Chapter 6

## Risk Monitoring and Control Process

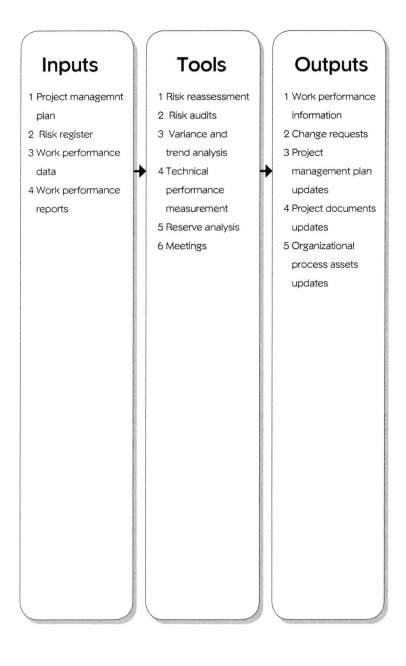

### Inputs
1 Project managemnt plan
2 Risk register
3 Work performance data
4 Work performance reports

### Tools
1 Risk reassessment
2 Risk audits
3 Variance and trend analysis
4 Technical performance measurement
5 Reserve analysis
6 Meetings

### Outputs
1 Work performance information
2 Change requests
3 Project management plan updates
4 Project documents updates
5 Organizational process assets updates

# Exercises to Remember Inputs, Outputs and Tools

Fill in the Blanks

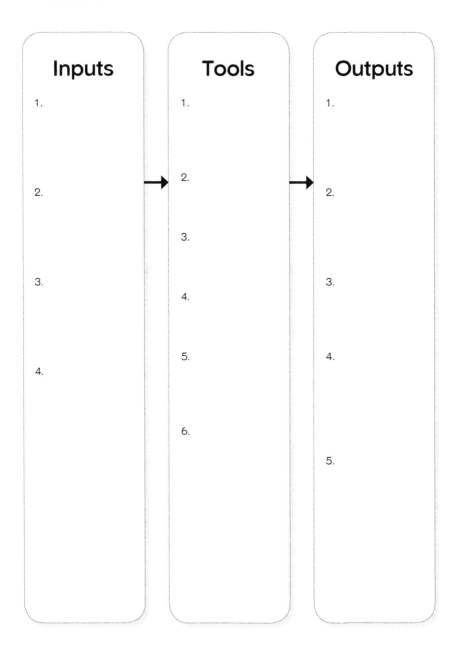

## Exercise 2

Now have another go at all the process at once.

**Risk Planning Process**

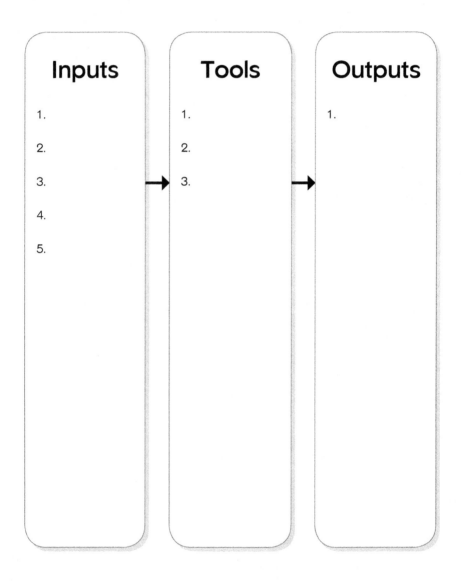

Exercises to Remember Inputs, Outputs and Tools

Risk Identification Process

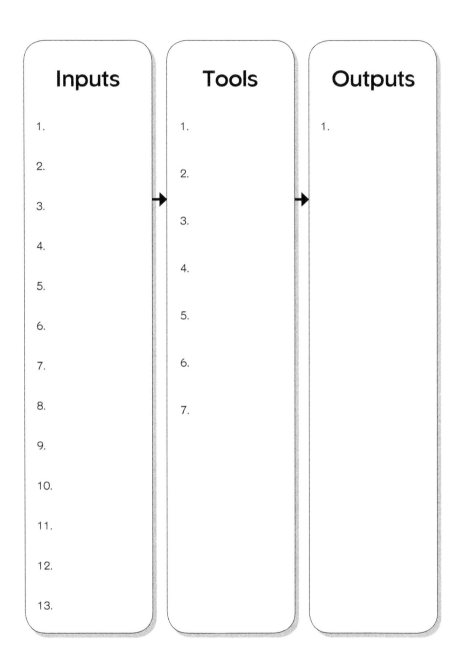

Chapter 6

## Risk Qualitative Analysis Process

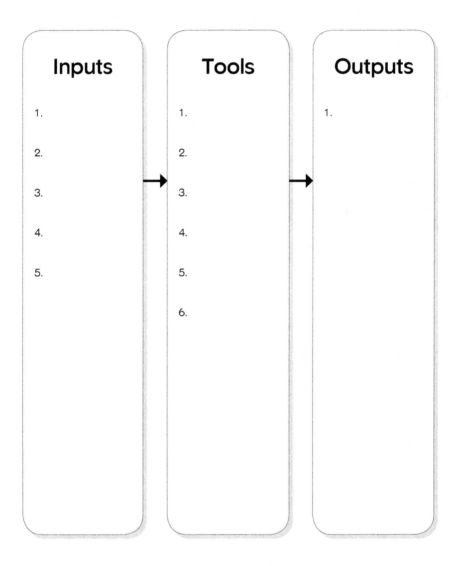

# Exercises to Remember Inputs, Outputs and Tools

Risk Quantitative Analysis Process

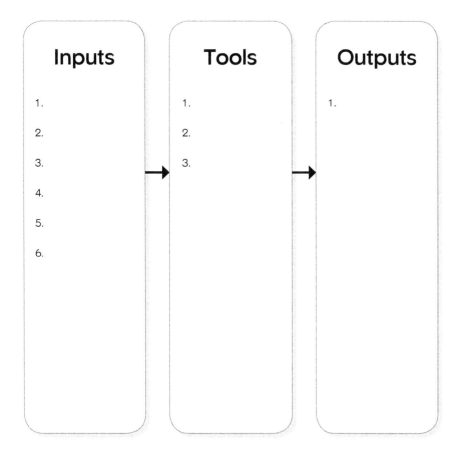

# Chapter 6

## Risk Response Planning Process

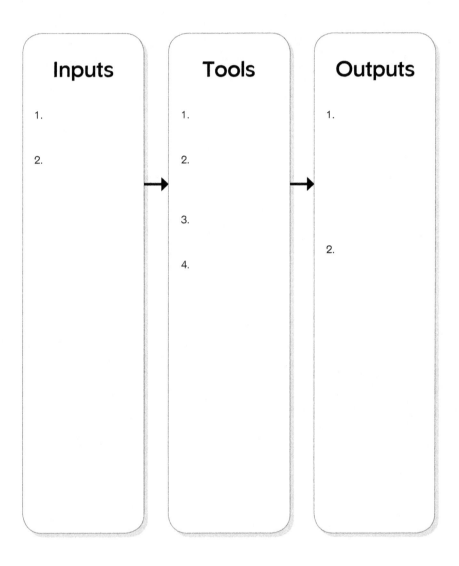

**Exercises to Remember Inputs, Outputs and Tools**

Risk Monitoring and Control Process

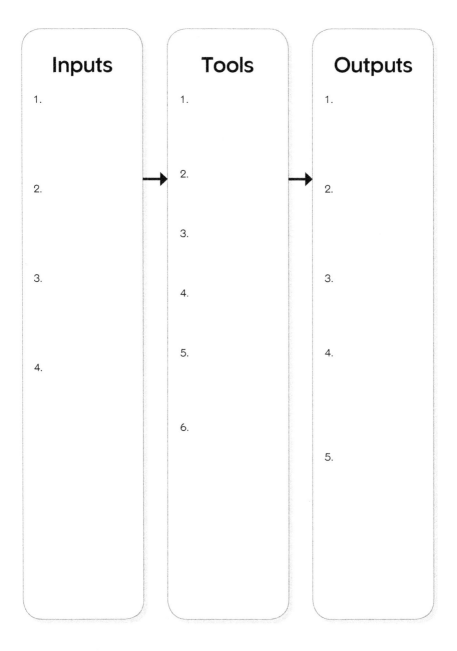

# Chapter 7:
# Risk Management Processes

Chapter 7

# Risk Management Processes

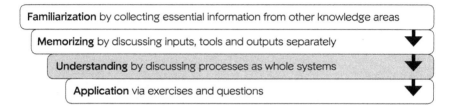

This chapter summarizes all aspects of the risk management processes. You will see the inputs, tools and outputs repeated here, but in the context of their respective processes. This chapter covers the core of the exam, and I hope that after you have gone through the previous chapters, you are now able to visualize the entire picture more easily. As no new concepts will be presented here, focus your efforts on understanding and linking the different elements together.

If you are able to go through this chapter with relative ease, then you are ready to take the practice test and move on to the RMP exam.

## Process One: Risk Planning

Risk management involves many activities and different tools and methods. You don't have to use all the tools, but rather identify what is best and appropriate for your project. The information presented in the PMBOK will guide you, but you are not expected to use each and every component of the processes. For example, there are different options (tools) that you may use for risk identification, yet it is not practical or even beneficial to try to use all of them. But how will you determine which tool to use? Who will be responsible for conducting risk management activities? These questions will all be answered in the risk planning process.

During risk planning, you will spend a good amount of time searching for information. Your goal is to align risk management for the project in hand with the company's procedures (e.g. by using approved templates).

Your goal in risk planning is similar to your goal in overall project planning; that is, to be efficient in the use of the resources of the project and to have a clear view of how you will proceed to achieve your objectives. In risk management, your objective is to control risks and minimize their negative impact on the project. Personally, I like to think of the objective as the act of producing a full and complete risk register and following its implementation in project execution. Having a plan is important to make you clearly focus on what you should be doing, what equipment you will need and who will participate with you at each stage.

Risk planning can take a few hours or a few days. It usually depends on the experience of the project team, the complexity of the project, the availability of information and the stakeholders level of tolerance.

### INPUTS

For risk planning process, you need to collect risk-relevant information on the project and the company. You can start with the project scope for you to know about the project's complexity and uniqueness. Then, you may go over the environmental factors and process assets to familiarize yourself with risk tolerance, and company risk procedures and templates. You also need to review the lessons learnt because this will help you avoid mistakes in risk planning that may have been encountered in earlier projects.

The following are the inputs you need to use as per the PMBOK:

| No. | Input | Description |
|---|---|---|
| 1 | Project management plan | The project plan is the "mother" of all the plans. You need to make it consistent and thus review it when preparing a plan for each of the 10 knowledge areas.<br>For example your risk activities will require time and budget, thus you should align any impacts with the cost and schedule plans. |
| 2 | Project charter | Usually big and clear (or high-level) risks are written in the charter. |
| 3 | Stakeholder register | The register will include information about your project stakeholders. It will help you decide on whom to invite |
| 4 | Enterprise environmental factors | From here, you will know the company's Level of risk tolerance. The lower the level of tolerance is; the more stringent risk Management should be. |
| 5 | Organizational process assets | From them you get the templates, risk Categories, definitions, etc. |

**Note:** *The list in the above table is a summary of each risk planning input. You need to refer to previous chapters for full details*

## TOOLS

PMBOK specifies only one tool for risk planning referred to as "meetings". Meetings are widely used for discussions and brainstorming. However, you need to control your meetings by having a clear agenda and by inviting the relevant people. Here, the experience of the project manager will help facilitate smoother and streamlined meetings; and your project will benefit from a dedicated risk manager.

# Risk Management Processes

| No. | Tools | Description |
|---|---|---|
| 1 | Analytical techniques | You analyze (i.e. think and try to understand) your stakeholders risk tolerance and the exposure to risks your project has. From that you can determine how much to invest in risk management ( for example, a low risk tolerance and high risk exposure will require stronger management of risks) |
| 2 | Expert judgment | A famous proverb says: "Give the bread dough to the baker even if he eats half of it. This simple sentence emphasize a collective wisdom in many cultures that no one can be smart in doing everything, and the smart person is the one who seek the expertise of others. So do the same in your project |
| 3 | Meetings | Meetings are used for discussions and brainstorming. You need to invite relevant people from your project team, stakeholders and the organization ( for example, if the company has a risk department you should invite them). |

**Note:** *Sometimes, a professional risk manager is appointed to projects. She/he reports to the project manager and is responsible for risk management. In the exam, you will see some questions using the term project manager and others, the term 'risk manager' and they should not affect your answer at all.*

**OUTPUTS**

Your output will be the risk management plan. This plan is a great way of communicating how you intend to conduct risk management. Ultimately, the risk management plan will be placed in the project plan before project execution starts.

| No. | Content of the Risk Plan | Description |
|---|---|---|
| 1 | Methodology | Defines how you will conduct risk management and what tools will be used. |
| 2 | Assignment of Roles | Defines who will do what. Example: who will call for meetings, take notes and share information. |
| 3 | Budgeting | If your risk management activities will cost you money, then you need to include that in the overall project cost. Example: you may hire an expert to conduct a one-day Delphi technique workshop. |
| 4 | Time | Defines when you are going to conduct risk identification, risk analysis, response and audits. |
| 5 | Risk Categories | Sources of risks are usually organized in an RBS. Does your company have one? You can use it to facilitate risk identification later. |
| 6 | Risk Matrix | Very important for defining the probabilities and impacts and for making your project team and stakeholders clear about them. Your risk matrix might be the single most important tool for risk analysis. |
| 7 | Stakeholders Tolerance | You will know about company tolerance from the enterprise environmental factors. However, you need to revise the tolerance for the specific project at hand. |
| 8 | Reporting and Tracking | Most of the communication can be done by sharing the updated risk register. You need to specify the information it will contain. During risk planning, you will also define how you will document and audit the implementation of risk management (for this task, it's usually better to appoint a risk manager). |

## Process two: Risk Identification

Risk identification will produce the list of risks that will be the basis for subsequent analysis. During risk planning, you identified the tools to use and assigned responsibilities for conducting meetings and workshops. You need to ensure good administration of the meetings by selecting the "right" people to attend and by taking minutes of meetings. Since you can choose from many different tools, you should brief the participants on the tool to be used and encourage a free exchange of information. You should identify the bulk of project risks at this stage, but, as you proceed in the project, you will most definitely identify more risks, so be prepared and be flexible.

### INPUTS

You will have many inputs in this process because you want to look for risks in all possible areas. However, you can logically guess inputs. For example, most of the risks will be related to either increased cost or delay, so you need to look at your cost and schedule plans and their estimations.

| No. | Inputs | Description |
| --- | --- | --- |
| 1 | Risk management plan | From now on, you will use the risk management plan as an input in the remaining processes. In this process, you will find useful information that will help you to identify risks like risk categories. |
| 2 | Cost management plan | Time, Money and Quality. A large percentage of any project risks will be related to these 3 areas. You should review the method used to develop these 3 in your project and how they will be controlled. You might discover errors. |
| 3 | Schedule management plan | |
| 4 | Quality management plan | |

| 5 | Human resource management plan | From the plan you can get the project organization structure, know about roles and responsibilities and staffing arrangements. |
|---|---|---|
| 6 | Scope baseline | You will find assumptions and the WBS. Both are important for identifying risks. |
| 7 | Activity cost estimates | You need to review the estimations that the project team already made for cost and time. Different techniques for estimations may be used and you should check for consistency and correctness. Wrong estimation for the duration or cost of a task is a source of risk. |
| 8 | Activity duration estimates | |
| 9 | Stakeholder register | You should use the register to select stakeholders who will participate at the various risk identification meetings. Also from the register, you can check if some stakeholders are missing. In addition, you can compare the stakeholders' requirements to the project objectives and identify possible conflicts. |
| 10 | Project documents | Such as logs, registers and method statements |
| 11 | Procurement documents | Here is a big source of risks. You need to make sure that such documents (like request for quotation) describe the service or product you intend to purchase in good details. Also you need to make sure such documents are consistent with the company policy. |

| 12 | Enterprise environmental factors | For risk identification, the more information you review, the better. Here, you will find information like risk attitude and published case studies. Depending on the time and resources, you can investigate the company more deeply to know about its cultural characteristics that may be sources of risks. For example, some companies have a "blame culture" where staff are blamed for mistakes and, as a result, are not encouraged to be innovative; or a "live and let live" culture that is characterized by complacency. |
|---|---|---|
| 13 | Organizational process assets | Here, you will find information like risk templates and procedures. In addition, you will find the lessons learnt from similar projects. |

## TOOLS

You have many tools for risk identification. However, they all follow the same basic concept of taking you systematically and step by step to logically see risks. Depending on your project scope and resources, you should select the appropriate tools and how many of them to use. Some tools are stronger than others; for example, from my experience, I found that brainstorming, when done thoroughly, will enable you to discover more than 75% of all risks.

Documentation Review during Risk Identification

| No. | Tools | Description |
|-----|-------|-------------|
| 1 | Documentation reviews | For your review to be considered a tool, it should be structured with a clear purpose and note taking, not just an ad hoc scan. |
| 2 | Checklist analysis | <ul><li>Brainstorming</li><li>Delphi Technique</li><li>Interviewing</li><li>Root Cause Analysis</li></ul> |
| 3 | Assumptions analysis | Here you use visual representations to stimulate your brain for identifying even more risks. You can use cause and effect charts, flowcharts and influence diagrams. |

# Risk Management Processes

| 4 | Diagramming techniques | Checklists give you a structure for identifying risks. You implement this tool by first selecting the right checklist for your project. Next, discuss with your team and stakeholders whether each risk mentioned in the checklist is applicable to the project at hand. You can find a variety of checklists; for example, you can find lists for risks in project management, construction, IT, communication, etc. You should not make this tool the only tool to use because it does not stimulate innovation in risk identification the way other tools - such as brainstorming - do. If you only use a checklist, then you run the risk of overlooking risks that are not mentioned in the list. Remember, the RBS is, basically, a checklist. |
|---|---|---|
| 5 | SWOT analysis | At the beginning of your project, you had expectations and made guesses. At the time of risk assessment, this could be many weeks ago, and it is a good idea to revisit them (this should encourage you to actually write your assumptions). |
| 6 | Expert judgment | Yet another way of finding risks... I like it because it lets me investigate the effect of the macro-environment on the project (the wider picture). Also, it encourages me to think of opportunities (i.e. positive risks). |
| 7 | Information gathering techniques | Expert opinions are powerful tools to be used in almost every process. Experts have developed senses that enable them to spot risks a mile away. They are the people who give you the simple solution that you often wonder: "why didn't I think of that". However, be aware of their bias, and, sometimes, overconfidence. |

## OUTPUTS

Now, you will create the risk register and will start continuous updating of it that will only end at the conclusion of the project itself.

| No. | Outputs | Description |
|-----|---------|-------------|
| 1 | Risk register | Your task here is to create the risk register and fill it with the identified risks. However, if you identify additional information such as possible responses to risks, you should still log them for further analysis in upcoming processes. Risk management is separated to identification, assessment and control for the purpose of simplification, but in real life you can do all three instantaneously in your mind. |

Example of a Risk Register Template

**Risk Register – Project XYZ**

Version Date

| No. | Risk | Effect on project | Probability | Impact | Risk Score | Strategy | Actions | By whom? | When? | Secondary Risks? | Risk State | Contingency Plan | Fall Back Plan | Reserve | Comments |
|-----|------|-------------------|-------------|--------|------------|----------|---------|----------|-------|------------------|------------|------------------|----------------|---------|----------|
| 001 | Delay in receiving equipment X | Delay of task Y | High | Medium | High | Mitigate | a) Close coordination with supplier  b) Look for other vendors | AAA | Date | N/A | Controlled | N/A | Use Equipment XX | NA | |
| 002 | | | | | | | | | | | | | | | |

## Process Three: Qualitative Risk Analysis

Risk Manager

At qualitative risk analysis process, you will arrange risks based on how much they can affect the project. In risk identification, you should adopt a "No Restriction" policy where you encourage the identification of all possible risks. Because of that, you are likely to discover many risks, but many of them will be of low impact on the project. Qualitative analysis will filter those risks (into a watch list) and pinpoint risks that are worthy of further analysis. This analysis has advantages of being relatively simple and fast and it usually yields good results. It is so useful that in many projects you are able to proceed to risk response right after doing qualitative risk analysis. However, this process is subjective since it depends on participants' opinions and experience. You should be particularly concerned with participants' biases.

The most widely used tool for this analysis is the risk matrix. It is easy to use and can foster a common understanding of the different levels of probability and impact. You can customize a risk matrix (to be more relaxed or stringent) based on the specific risk tolerance for the project.

# Chapter 7

**INPUTS**

| No. | Inputs | Description |
|---|---|---|
| 1 | Risk management plan | You will find useful information like the risk matrix and risk tolerance. |
| 2 | Scope baseline | Basically it will tell you what is your project. If the scope is similar to other projects that were done before then you can use some of the assessment already done. Not to copy and past but also not to start from scratch |
| 3 | Risk register | To know the list of identified risks |
| 4 | Enterprise environmental factors | You can find industry specific risks and checklists. For example, if you have a project to host a marathon in your city, then referring to agencies like the international marathon racers should provide valuable information about risks in such projects. |
| 5 | Organizational process assets | Here, you will find the lessons learnt. Knowing the effect of risks on similar projects can help you guess their possible effect on the current project. |

# Risk Management Processes

## TOOLS

| No. | Tools | Description |
|---|---|---|
| 1 | Probability and impact matrix | These two tools are closely related. You use a matrix to assess your probabilities and impact. The risk matrix is the main tool in risk qualitative analysis. You can invite stakeholders to a risk analysis meeting, give each one a copy of the risk matrix and go though each risk to assess its chance of happening and effect on the project. This is the main tool in risk qualitative analysis. You can invite stakeholders to a risk analysis meeting, give each one a copy of the risk matrix and go though each risk to assess its chances of occuring and effect on the project. |
| 2 | Risk probability and impact assessment | |
| 3 | Risk data quality assessment | This should be done at the beginning. It basically refers to the level of confidence in the collected information about risks. For example, if a risk is said to have happened in previous projects, you need to be confident of that as a fact. |
| 4 | Risk categorization | If you have many risks, say in the hundreds, you can use the RBS to group risks by source. Thus, you can better rank them relative to each other. Note, that I said "if", meaning you have to option to use it. Just emphasizing the fact that you don't need to use all the tools. |
| 5 | Risk urgency assessment | You rank the risks based on how soon in the project they are likely to happen. You can use the project schedule to help you in this. Urgent risks should be ranked higher than others. |
| 6 | Expert judgment | For example, you may invite a civil engineering professor to your one-of-a kind construction project. He should help you more in understanding and ranking technical risks. However, be careful of biases by asking experts to justify their opinions as much as possible. |

## OUTPUTS

| No. | outputs | | Description |
|---|---|---|---|
| 1 | Project documents updates | Risk Register Updates | • The risk register will include:<br>• . List of ranked risks<br>• . List of risks with low impact on the project (watch list)<br>• . Risks grouped by their sources<br>• . Risks ranked based on their urgency |
| 2 | | Assumptions log updates | Chances are you made assumptions in your project because enough information weren't available. For example, you assumed that the cost of shipping will increase by 5% due to a tornado somewhere. However with time information came that the tornado wasn't as bad and shipping costs will not be affected. Such assumptions need to be updated. Remember that assumptions are recorded in a separate log. |

### Process Four: Quantitative Risk Analysis

In this process, you will use mathematics and statistics to predict the potential effect of risks on your project. I still remember one of my professors during my master's studies telling me "No one can argue with numbers"- if they were developed correctly. To complement the above statement, I recall another professor who taught me simulation to say that whenever he presented a simulation run to a company, they immediately asked him to work for them. Nowadays, there are different risk simulation software that can aid you in quantitative analysis. Presenting results from simulation can help you secure stakeholders' support. Consider the case where you want to secure additional funds for your project from the sponsor, which one of the following statements is more likely to get you what you want?

# Risk Management Processes

**Statement 1:** The project has many risks and I think we will face troubles finishing on budget. I believe we need to add **x** amount of money to be on the safe side.

**Statement 2:** After hundreds of simulation runs, the chance of achieving the project on budget is 60%. We need to add **x** amount of money to raise the chances to 90%.

The second statement is more convincing, since it sounds more reasonable and scientific. The first statement, however, has words like "I think" and "I believe", and for every "I think" there is another "I think" that is equal in magnitude and opposite in direction (the law of "I think"!!!).

Quantitative risk analysis is relatively expensive and time consuming. Many small projects do not go through it, and for their scope, it might be perfectly fine to do only the qualitative assessment.

## INPUTS

| No. | Inputs | Description |
|---|---|---|
| 1 | Risk management plan | By now, you know that the risk management plan is a place for miscellaneous (different) information that you need to consult in each process. Here, you may want to review the definitions of probability and impact you set for your current project. |
| 2 | Cost management plan | On these plans, you will base your modeling and simulation |
| 3 | Schedule management plan | |
| 4 | Risk register | In the risk register, you will find the list of prioritized risks (as the quantitative assessment is relatively expensive, you need to be selective of which risks need further analysis). |

| | | | |
|---|---|---|---|
| 5 | Enterprise environmental factors | | You might find specific studies for your type of project. For example, specialized risk data on oil fire if your project involves works on oil pipelines. |
| 6 | Organizational process assets | | For the lessons learnt. |

**TOOLS**

| No. | Tools | | Description |
|---|---|---|---|
| 1 | Data gathering and representation techniques | Interview | You interview experts to get different estimates on risk impact. |
| | | Probability Distribution | These are used to represent the probability of risk events in ranges of continuous numbers. These representations are used, in turn, in simulation. |
| 2 | Quantitative risk analysis and modeling techniques | Sensitivity Analysis | To find risks that have the biggest effect on the project. |
| | | Expected Monetary Value | Use it to find expected impact of different risk scenarios on the project. |
| | | Modeling and Simulation | Used to virtually run the project many times on a computer, utilizing the Monte Carlo technique. |
| 3 | Expert judgment | | In quantitative analysis, you use many statistical and mathematical techniques. You should seek the advice of experts on them as needed (for example, to properly analyze and interpret the outcome of a simulation run). |

## OUTPUTS

| No. | Outputs | Description |
|---|---|---|
| 1 | Project documents updates (risk register updates) | • Now, the risk register will include information on the expected completion date and cost. This information will help you add time and money contingency reserves.<br>• The risk register will include the overall probability of achieving the project objectives.<br>• The list of prioritized risks will be improved and fine tuned.<br>• Any new insights. Since you are using modeling and computers can generate different possible outputs you might find a trend or some abnormalities that catches your attention. For example, after running a simulation model for 50 times you noticed that the project fails to meet one task on 80% of the runs. You need to think on how to improve on that by looking at what risks might cause that failure and how to control it. |

## Process Five: Risk Response Planning

> Remember, risks can be positive or negative

This is the last risk management process before you start project execution. Let's see what we have so far: a risk register that was created and updated in the previous processes. The project team, and the stakeholders have come a long way and if they stop now, they have achieved some success, such as having developed an adequate understanding of the risks involved. Have you seen how important risk management is? By now, a communication plan has been established and reviewed; stakeholders have been involved; and experts have been consulted. All of this has a positive impact on the project. However, if we stop now, we will be missing the opportunity of controlling the risks (which many times, require little or no money to control; since some risks can be controlled through changing work methods or enhancing communication). Unfortunately, although many project managers take risk identification seriously, they come up short when it comes to risk response. Risk response should be very innovative. Think of it as a problem solving exercise where there are different options from which you can choose to control each risk.

Personally, I like this process because I can use risk management terminology. Not everyone will know the meaning of mitigation or exploiting, let alone applying such concepts. This helps overthrow the idea that people can be risk managers overnight and supports the importance of learning and practicing risk management.

# Risk Management Processes

Within this risk response planning process, you will specify the risk owners. In risk planning, you assigned responsibilities for undertaking different risk activities, but, here, you will identify people who will be responsible for controlling the actual risks. You need a "name" to avoid blame throwing between different parties. Even if many parties are involved in controlling a risk, it should all boil down to only one responsible person. Risk owners need to be identified in a logical manner and you should select the one who has the most adequate resources and authority to control the risks. In addition, risk owners need to be communicated with and their formal acceptance has to be secured.

## INPUTS

| No. | Inputs | Description |
|---|---|---|
| 1 | Risk management plan | Contains the important information such as risk definitions. |
| 2 | Risk register | You need the risk register for the list of risks and their ranking, for risks that are urgent, and for any initial response that you specified during the risk identification process. |

## TOOLS

You should not rush assigning response strategies. You have different tools available for use and you should find the one that is most effective for controlling the identified risks, and at the same time, the one that is cost effective.

| No. | Tools | Description |
|---|---|---|
| 1 | Strategies for negative risks or threats | Avoid, transfer, mitigate and accept. |
| 2 | Strategies for positive risks or opportunities | Exploit, share, enhance and accept. |
| 3 | Contingent response strategies | Contingency planning is a strategy for designing a plan to deal with a risk if it happens. Think of it as an emergency plan that you put on a shelf to use later if needed. You need early warning signs of risks (called triggers) to be able to get ready to use the plan. |
| 4 | Expert judgment | You might encounter some risks that are unique and you have no previous experience dealing with them. Thus, you will need to consult experts regarding such risks. This situation is very common in innovative projects. Experts are available within the company and outside it, and with the Internet, the list is always expanding and accessible. |

**OUTPUT**

| No. | Output | Description |
|---|---|---|
| 1 | Project management plan Updates | Responses will definitely affect some of your project plan sections. You might need to update the cost plan, schedule plan, quality plan, HR plan, etc. CHANGE REQUESTs are needed if such changes are required so the overall unity of the project plan is not compromised. |
| 2 | Project documents updates | . Risk Register: You will update the risk register by including information about the risk responses and who owns them, triggers, secondary risks, the contingency reserve, residual risks and fallback plans.<br>. Assumption log: As you design responses, assumptions would be challenged and changed.<br>. Technical documents, like method statements, drawings, electrical requirements, etc.<br>. Contract Decisions: During risk response, you may transfer or share risks. You need to reflect these decisions in your contract. |

# Risk Management Processes

## Some Terminology

Make sure you know the following terms, as this will help you answer many questions correctly.

| No. | Term | What it is |
|---|---|---|
| 1 | Risk Response Strategies | They are steps that you take to control risks during the project planning phase. They apply to threats and opportunities. |
| 2 | Triggers | Early warnings of risks. |
| 3 | Fallback Plan | Plan "B", which is to be implemented if the primary plan to control the risk fails. |
| 4 | Contingency Plans | A plan that you implement if a risk occurs during project execution. |
| 5 | Contingency Reserve | Money or time assigned to deal with accepted risks, if they occur. |
| 6 | Risk Owners | People who will implement the risk control. |
| 7 | Workarounds | They are actions that you take if unplanned risks occur. Here, both the risk and actions are not planned. |
| 8 | Watch List | Risks that are low in magnitude and do not require a response, but need to be monitored. |
| 9 | Secondary Risks | Risks that are generated from implementing the risk response. |
| 10 | Residual Risks | Risks that still remain after risk response measures have been implemented. |
| 11 | Passive Acceptance | To accept a risk without a contingency reserve. |
| 12 | Active Acceptance | To accept a risk with a contingency reserve. |

# Chapter 7

The figure below summarizes the options you may take to deal with risks. It is more like my personal "mental map", and I advise you to make your own.

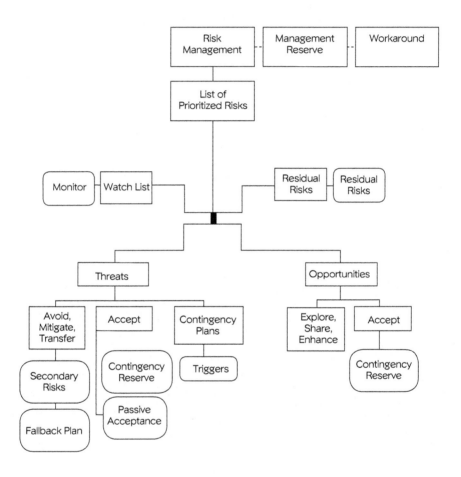

Make your own diagram on risk response options (start with the list of prioritized risks):

Chapter 7

### Process Six: Risk Monitoring and Control

This is the last process in project risk management as per the PMI's PMBOK. In this process, you might add newly identified risks and delete ones that did not happen. Also, as the project unfolds, risks might require reassessment. You should establish close communication with the risk owners who look after the implementation of the response strategies. A thing to remember is that this process, unlike the others, is done during project execution, and thus, has special characteristics. For example, changes and modifications on how to respond to new risks must be done through change requests.

Do not forget your watch list, residual risks and triggers. You need to monitor all of them actively. A key element in this process is performance reporting, which is the means to know how efficiently (or inefficiently) you are doing.

You need to be open-minded here. Expect that not all identified risks will happen. Also, be prepared for new risks. Be prepared to implement a fallback plan if the original response fails, and utilize your contingency reserve as needed.

## Risk Management Processes

**INPUTS**

| No. | Input | Description |
|---|---|---|
| 1 | Project management plan | Actually, you will be using the risk management plan, but since you started project execution, it has been incorporated in the overall project plan. You will find information on risk tolerance and risk management methods used. You need to refer to the risk methods as you might discover new risks and thus want to repeat risk management. |
| 2 | Risk register | The register will include the risks, their owners and response actions. Also, it will contain the watch list, fallback plans, triggers, contingency reserve, secondary risks, etc. |
| 3 | Work performance data | As you are in the project execution phase, you need to know how well you are performing. One of your objectives in this process is to validate how effective your risk management has been. Good performance implies good risk management. As for the performance reports, they provide you with analyses on performance information, such as trend analysis and earned value calculations (in essence, performance reports explain performance information). |
| 4 | Work performance reports | |

## TOOLS

| No. | Tools | Description |
|-----|-------|-------------|
| 1 | Risk reassessment | Sometimes, you need to reassess risks as follows:<br>• You might discover new risks<br>• Conditions change in the project so that risks might lose or gain magnitude (in terms of probability and impact)<br>• Risks might not happen and, hence, need to be closed<br>Reassessment should be done regularly as changes in risk continue. Be careful in the exam, do not confuse assessment with reassessment! |
| 2 | Risk audits | Risk audits check the effectiveness of your risk management. You may use templates and involve some stakeholders with you. For example, you may check the risk response on a randomly selected risk from the risk register by contacting the risk owner and asking for feedback. |
| 3 | Variance and trend analysis | Trends about past performance can indicate how effective your risk management is. For example, you can compute the expected budget at project completion using the earned value method. If the expected budget is very close to your planned one, it indicates good risk management (meaning your work of risk planning, identification, analysis and response was excellent). On the other hand, if you find much variance between the planned performance and actual performance, it might trigger you to revisit your risk register and validate it (i.e. validate the list of risks and the effectiveness of response actions). |

| 4 | Technical performance measurement | Good technical performance in your project also implies sound risk management and control. Consider a project of constructing an undersea oil pipeline. Your technical specifications here might be for the quality of welding on the pipe joints and the number of areas where welding failed. You should have identified failed welding as a risk and put response actions to control it, and if the number of defects is accepted, it implies good risk management. |
|---|---|---|
| 5 | Reserve analysis | This analysis compares how many risks are remaining to the amount of the remaining reserve. Based on the analysis, you may want to increase or decrease the reserve. If you fail to balance the reserve with risks, you might not have sufficient funds to control some of the accepted risks. |
| 6 | Meetings | You use meetings to interactively discuss risk responses with your project team and stakeholders. |

## OUTPUTS

Outputs here are either updates to documents or change requests.

| No. | Outputs | Description |
|---|---|---|
| 1 | Work performance information | • After applying the risk control tools, you should know how performance was affected. This should be communicated and assessed for taking future decisions. |
| 2 | Change requests | • During project planning, you identified risk responses and updated the project management plan to reflect any changes. However, during project execution, changes need to be controlled via change requests. Change requests dealing with risk management can be either 'preventive' or 'corrective' actions.<br>• You use preventive actions to prevent risks from happening (i.e. new risks identified through risk reassessment).<br>• On the other hand, you use corrective actions for risks that already happened and you want to reduce their impact on the project. For example, if an unplanned risk happens, you should work around it, and this involves actions that are not specified in the project plan, and thus, must go through a change request/approval process. Another example is implementing a contingency plan, where, although the risks are identified, response actions are simply documented in a contingency plan but are not incorporated in the project plan. They still need to go through a change request process. Expect a few questions on this topic, so read the statements above as you need to have good grasp on this topic. |

# Risk Management Processes

| | | |
|---|---|---|
| 3 | Project management plan updates | Implementing change requests will most likely affect some elements of the project plan such as the schedule, cost, quality or HR plans. These changes need to be documented. |
| 4 | Project documents updates (risk Register updates) | The risk register will contain new information like:<br>• The actual outcome of risks and the effectiveness of the risk response<br>• New risks and their analysis<br>• Updates to previously identified risks, based on risk reassessment |
| 5 | Organizational process assets updates | Remember, we used organizational process assets to find information about the risk matrix, risk categories and lessons learnt. Now, as the project has been closed, you have learned new information and it is time to practice knowledge management and feed this into the organizational assets. For example, you may update:<br>• The Lessons Learnt Database<br>• The Risk Breakdown Structure (with new risks)<br>• Company templates |

Chapter 7

***Final Note:*** *Having a full set of risk management documentation will not control risks in itself. You need to implement what is inside those documents.*

Risk Management Process

# Chapter 8:
# Practice Questions

Chapter 8

# Practice Questions

**Before you take the exam**

- Enter www.pmi.org and make sure the exam structure did not change. Check the scope of the exam, duration and number of questions.
- Schedule for the exam in advance. Usually, there is a huge demand on the testing center as they provide different types of exams.
- Read the testing center policies regarding canceling or changing the exam date. However, I strongly advise you not to get into the habit of delaying the exam. A friend of mine delayed his exam more than 5 times and only took it because the deadline for taking the exam was going to end (from the time of registering, you have one year to take the exam).
- I advise you not to take more than one month from the time you start studying to the time of taking the exam.
- Think about your strategy. Are you going to answer all the questions at once or mark difficult ones to come back to later? Also, are you going to read the given answer choices before you read the question? Personally, I like to read the given answers in reverse order (starting from 'd' to 'a') as it helped me avoid rushing in my selection.
- Psyche up, this might be the most useful pre-exam advice I can provide you. Set your mind to "exam mode". Accept that you will benefit from the exam. Acknowledge the fact that it will be challenging and know that you will encounter trick questions. This will help you avoid panicking.
- Remember, the good old exam advice: have a good night's sleep, don't overeat, wake up early and avoid traffic.

**About the Questions**

- Remember, you have 170 questions to answer in 3.5 hours.
- Questions can be divided into two types: short and straightforward, and long scenario-based questions. For the scenario-based questions, it will help if you refer to your own experience and ask yourself: what would I do if I am faced with this situation in real life?
- There will be some tricky and difficult questions. However, they are tricky for those who are inexperienced with risk management. I urge you to view difficult questions as a positive thing because they will filter out those people with insufficient experience in risk management. Many people can

just read about risk management, but reading alone is not sufficient for one to be called a "Risk Management Professional".
- In answering the questions, you should always analyze the given problem and identify the basic cause. Many times, in scenario-based questions, you will not be given full information and will be required to look for the BEST solution. By BEST, I mean you need to compare all the given answers and identify the one that best fits the situation. For example, you might find two answers that will solve a given scenario, but one of them should be done BEFORE the other, therefore, the former has to be given more weight.

## Question Types

In the exam, you will have a variety of questions. The following is a discussion of some.

### Mathematical Questions

In the exam, you will find questions asking you to make simple calculations. You should remember some of the simple formulas like the number of communication channels and the three-point estimation. Also, familiarize yourself with the built-in calculator. Be careful, as some questions might give you "extra" information, like numbers that you don't need to use to find the answer. Mathematical questions are usually straightforward, unlike other questions.

### Questions on Communication

Communication is of prime importance in the exam. This is expected since improper communication can cause many risks in real life. Remember that the communication plan guides you on how to send information and to whom to send it. In addition, a major responsibility of the project manager is to identify stakeholder requirements, try to achieve them and resolve any issues.

### Questions on Where to Find Information

A great deal of your work as a risk professional involves searching for information. Expect to see many questions asking where to look for certain information. To answer those questions, you should be familiar with the inputs and with what they contain. For example, if I ask you where to find work packages, you should know that they are inside the WBS, which is inside the scope baseline. Try the following matching exercise that tests your understanding of different inputs and what they contain.

# Chapter 8

**Exercise:** Match the elements from the two columns (on the right and left) with risk management inputs in the middle column.

|  |  |  |
|---|---|---|
| | Activity Cost Estimation | |
| Hourly Cost of a Pipefitter | Activity Duration Estimation | Risk Matrix |
| Time Ranges of Task Durations | Project scope statement | Urgent Risks |
| Project Budget | Cost Plan | Secondary Risks |
| Milestones | Schedule Plan | Adjustment Rate for Inflation |
| RBS - company | Communication Plan | Residual Risks |
| Risk Tolerance for the Project at hand | Enterprise Environmental Factors | Assumptions |
| | Organizational Process Assets | WBS |
| Scope Statement | Risk Management Plan | Possible Root Cause |
| Stakeholders Requirements and Contact Information | Scope Baseline | Stakeholders Register |
| | Stakeholders Register | Management Reserve |
| Earned Value Information | Quality Plan | Fallback Plans |
| Quality Specifications | Project Documents | Industry Studies |
| Contingency Reserve | Performance Reports | RBS - Project |
| Cost Performance Index | Performance Information | Network Diagram |
| Project Status | | Method Used for Developing Project Schedule |
| Watch List | | |
| Possible Responses to Risks | | Lessons Learnt |
| List of Risks | | Templates |
| Risk Ranking | Risk Register - After Risk Identification | Basic Causes of Risks |
| Probabilistic Impact of Risks | Risk Register - After Qualitative Analysis | Outcome of Predicted Risks |
| Response Strategies | | Risk Tolerance – For the Company |
| Risk Owners | Risk Register – After Qualitative Analysis | |
| Project Deliverables | | Information Distribution |
| | Risk Register – After Risk Response | Registers, Logs, Metrics, etc. |
| | Risk Register – Project End | |

You will find the answers to the exercise in the table below. Note that the risk register is a special input and its contents will vary depending on what risk management process you are in. You should be careful here as some information can first appear in one process, but be fully developed in another. Take, for example, the root causes of risks: they are available in the risk register after you finish the qualitative analysis, but they might also be available in a basic form after you finish risk identification.

## Practice Questions

| Input | Information |
|---|---|
| Activity Cost Estimation | • Hourly Cost of a Pipefitter<br>• Adjustment Rate for Inflation |
| Activity Duration Estimation | • Time ranges of task(s) durations |
| Project Scope Statement | • Project Deliverables<br>• Assumptions |
| Cost Plan | • Project Budget<br>• Management Reserve<br>• Method Used in Developing Project Cost |
| Schedule Management Plan | • Milestones<br>• Network Diagram |
| Communication Management Plan | • Information Distribution |
| Enterprise Environmental Factors | • Risk Tolerance for the whole Company<br>• Industry Studies |
| Organizational Process Assets | • RBS – for the whole company<br>• Templates<br>• Risk Matrix<br>• Lessons Learnt<br>• Stakeholder Register |
| Risk Management Plan | • RBS - Project<br>• Risk Tolerance for the Project at hand |
| Scope Baseline | • Scope Statement<br>• WBS |
| Stakeholders Register | • Stakeholders List, Requirements and Contact Details |
| Quality Plan | • Quality Specification |
| Project Documents | • Registers, Logs, Metrics, etc. |
| Performance Reports | • Earned Value Information<br>• Cost Performance Index<br>• Schedule Performance Index |
| Performance Information | • Project Status |
| Risk Register – After Risk Identification | • List of Risks<br>• Possible Root Causes<br>• Possible Responses |
| Risk Register – After Qualitative Assessment | • Risk Ranking<br>• Watch List<br>• Urgent Risks<br>• Basic Causes of Risks |
| Risk Register – After Quantitative Assessment | • Probabilistic Impact of Risks |
| Risk Register – After Risk Response | • Response Strategies<br>• Risk Owners<br>• Residual Risks<br>• Contingency Reserve<br>• Secondary Risks<br>• Fallback Plans |
| Risk Register – Project End | Outcome of Predicted Risks |

From the above table, I can make at least 40 different straightforward questions.

### Note about the Sample Questions in this Book

- My intention is not to give you 170 questions (as in the real exam), but to cover all possible concepts that the exam authors can use to generate questions from.
- I will try to give a variety of the same question.
- I follow different approaches in analyzing questions. Sometimes I analyze them in a table and sometimes I just discuss them in paragraph form.

### Before You Start with the Questions

In the exam, you will be given some scratch papers. I advise you to draw the six risk processes on one of them as soon as you can. It will help reduce doubts, improve your speed of answering many questions and make you more confident overall. So, let's put this into practice and prepare a "cheat sheet" and use it for the practice questions.

# Questions

# Chapter 8

**Question 1:** An experienced risk manager was assigned to handle a very innovative bridge building project. The project involves building a bridge with three levels, one for cars, one for trucks and one for a train. The risk manager calculated the chance of finishing the project within the $900 million budget to be only 65%. When he revealed this information to the major stakeholders, the sponsor was worried and asked him how he came up with such figures. What technique did the risk manager use?

a) Monte Carlo Simulation
b) Expert Judgment
c) The S-Curve
d) Lessons Learnt

**Question 2:** What is an output of the risk monitoring and control process?

a) Control Charts
b) New Risk Register Template
c) Risk Owners List
d) Company Risk Probability and Impact Definitions

**Question 3:** What is the best way of communicating information?

a) Push
b) Pull
c) Interactive
d) Confidential

# Practice Questions

**Question 4:** You are the risk manager of a major BPR project in your municipality (BPR = Business Process Re-engineering). Before starting on risk response planning, you receive a phone call from one of the major stakeholders asking if he can look at the initial risk responses. Where can you find this information?

a) Risk Register – After Risk Planning
b) Risk Register – After Risk Identification
c) Risk Register – After Risk Response
d) Risk Register – After Risk Analysis

**Question 5:** For the numbers: 2.3, 4, 6.5, 6 and 7, the mean is:

a) 5
b) 5.2
c) 5.4
d) 5.25

**Question 6:** Risks that are generated as a direct result of implementing risk responses are called:

a) Watch Risks
b) Secondary Risks
c) Residual Risks
d) Primary Risks

**Question 7:** You just finished updating the risk register and added the names of risk owners. What risk management process was just completed?

a) Identifying Risks
b) Performing Qualitative Risk Analysis
c) Performing Quantitative Risk Analysis
d) Planning Risk Response

**Question 8:** You are the risk manager in a consultancy project to provide an electronic archiving system for a large municipality. Many concerns about risks preoccupy your mind and you want to have a proper analysis to address them. For the very same reason, you will use a technique to get a consensus from the stakeholders on these risks. What process are you at?

a) Plan Risk Management
b) Identify Risks
c) Perform Qualitative Risk Analysis
d) Perform Quantitative Risk Analysis

**Question 9:** For a change, you will write the question for the multiple choices below. Make a story about a multinational project and the correct answer should be 'd'. My claim is that when you put yourself in the place of the exam authors, you will be tempted to think like them and will gain more insight on how to solve more questions.

Write the question here : ----------------------------------------------------------------
--------------------------------------------------------------------------------
--------------------------------------------------------------------------------

a) Informal
b) Informal - Written
c) Informal - Verbal
d) Formal Language

Explain why answer 'd' is selected: -----------------------------------------------
--------------------------------------------------------------------------------
--------------------------------------------------------------------------------

Practice Questions

**Question 10:** The project sponsor asked you, as the project manager, to provide information about the effectiveness of risk management in project delivery. He has requested you to provide this information to some other stakeholders as well. What method should the project manager use to deliver this information?

a) Emails
b) Presentation
c) Reports
d) Phone calls

**Question 11:** During a risk identification meeting, some stakeholders did not show up. What should the project manager do?

a) Check the communication plan
b) Just send them the minutes of the meeting
c) Don't invite them to upcoming meetings
d) Send an email to tell them that they have missed the meeting and ask them to
   attend future meetings

**Question 12:** --------- is called risk mitigation.

a) Decreasing the probability of the occurrence of a risk
b) Ensuring that a risk will never occur
c) Sharing the benefits of an opportunity
d) Transferring the risk to a third party

## Chapter 8

**Question 13:** Using improper body language can be a dangerous:

a) Communication Stopper
b) Communication Blocker
c) Communication Hindrance
d) Communication Virus

**Question 14:** You are conducting risk planning and would like to know about risk tolerance. Where do you find this information?

a) Risk Management Plan
b) Risk Register – After Risk Identification
c) Enterprise Environmental Factors
d) Organizational Process Assets

**Question 15:** As the IT services section head in your company, you were assigned to run a project to internally develop a software for the financial department. You identified the need to assign external programmers on short contracts and budgeted that in your cost plan. During risk identification, one of your project team members was worried it would take a lengthy procedure to hire the programmers. To determine how long the procedures could take, you should look in:

a) Project Scope Statement
b) Project Scope Baseline
c) Enterprise Environmental Factors
d) Organizational Process Assets

# Practice Questions

**Question 16:** Here, you will have to write the question. Make a scenario about a risk manager working in a major project. Mention that the project manager is using a tool that is part of risk monitoring and control. Ask what process the risk manager is involved in. The correct answer should be 'd' from the list below. Give additional information that is irrelevant in order to distract the reader from the correct answer.

Write the question here ---------------------------------------------------------------
------------------------------------------------------------------------------------------
------------------------------------------------------------------------------------------
------------------------------------------------------------------------------------------
------------------------------------------------------------------------------------------
------------------------------------------------------------------------------------------
------------------------------------------------------------------------------------------
------------------------------------------------------------------------------------------

a) Plan Risk Management
b) Identify Risks
c) Perform Qualitative Risk Analysis
d) Monitor and Control Risks

Write your reasoning behind selecting answer 'd' here ----------------------------
------------------------------------------------------------------------------------------
------------------------------------------------------------------------------------------
------------------------------------------------------------------------------------------
------------------------------------------------------------------------------------------
------------------------------------------------------------------------------------------
------------------------------------------------------------------------------------------
------------------------------------------------------------------------------------------
------------------------------------------------------------------------------------------
------------------------------------------------------------------------------------------

## Chapter 8

**Question 17:** During the planning phase of a project to develop a software, you (the risk manager) identified a risk involving how the insufficient number of programmers may delay a critical task in the project. The response made and implemented was to hire one additional programmer to mitigate the risk. However, while implementing the critical task, you realized that you need another programmer. What should you do?

a) Contact the local recruitment agency to recruit a programmer ASAP
b) Issue a change request (corrective action) to hire a new programmer
c) Issue a change request (preventive action) to hire a new programmer
d) As the project execution has started there is nothing that can be done

**Question 18:** You have been assigned to manage a project of building a big fountain in the middle of the city. You and the project team are reviewing the quality plan to identify risks. One of your team members tells you that the lighting specifications might not meet the requirements of the well-connected local "Green Community Club". How can you verify the information shared by the team member?

a) You need to review the stakeholders register
b) You need to review the communication plan
c) You need to review the quality plan
d) You can ignore the matter, as community clubs cannot affect the project

## Practice Questions

**Question 19:** You are the project manager of a tunnel-digging project. The project is divided into many sections. In one section of the tunnel, you may choose between two paths, the first is shorter but might contain harder rocks. Taking Path 1 will cost you
$1 million, and if you encounter hard rocks you need to allocate more resources to digging, which will cost you an additional $200,000. The chance of encountering hard rocks is 45%. Path 2 is longer and it will cost $1.1 million to dig up. However, the chance of encountering hard rocks is estimated by the geologist to be only 15%. The cost of digging up hard rocks is the same for Path 1. Which path should you choose?

a) Path 1
b) Path 2
c) Path 1 and 2 are the same in terms of monetary value
d) Cannot decide as more information is needed

**Question 20:** You are the risk manager of a project to build a small oil platform in the middle of the sea. This kind of project is very dangerous and there is a high chance of workers getting injured. If a worker is injured, the project will be delayed (since investigations will have to be performed to ensure the safety of other workers). You are able to convince the project manager to hire two dedicated safety engineers for the project in addition to the safety engineers provided by subcontractors. What type of risk strategy is this?

a) Risk Avoidance
b) Risk Transfer
c) Risk Mitigation
d) Risk Acceptance

# Chapter 8

**Question 21:** As a risk manager, you made a plan to fast track your project if there was any delay in an important task. Missing some milestones will trigger you to implement the plan. This plan is called:

a) Trigger Plan
b) Contingency Plan
c) Contingency Reserve Plan
d) Fallback Plan

**Question 22:** You are the project manager of a large project; your team is largely made of fresh graduates, what leadership style is the BEST to use in this context?

a) Laissez-faire Leadership
b) Democratic Leadership
c) Autocratic Leadership
d) People Oriented Leadership

**Question 23:** You are a member of a project that is organized to launch a new home appliance product. You noticed that the project manager had some strange behavior. In one instance, he visited your office after the weekend and spent one hour asking you what you did in the weekend. In another occasion, you went to visit him to discuss the communication plan of the project but he tried to make the discussion short and you felt that he did not give the subject enough attention. What leadership style best describes the project manager's behavior?

a) Laissez-faire Leadership
b) Democratic Leadership
c) Autocratic Leadership
d) People Oriented Leadership

## Practice Questions

**Question 24:** In which risk management process can the risk manager provide top management with information on the possibility of meeting the overall objectives of the project?

a) Quantitative Risk Analysis
b) Qualitative Risk Analysis
c) Simulation Risk Analysis
d) Overall Risk Analysis

**Question 25:** You are managing a worker satisfaction project in an organization with a matrix structure. You are facing difficulties getting the required help from one of the functional managers. The functional manager would like to see some proofs of your authority in the project. Where can you find such information?

a) Scope Statement
b) Scope Baseline
c) Risk Management Plan
d) Project Charter

**Question 26:** What is the strategy to use when you come across benefits that you are unable to utilize?

a) Exploit
b) Share
c) Enhance
d) Transfer

# Chapter 8

**Question 27:** During risk planning you decided to use assumption analysis to identify risks. Where should you search for assumptions?

a) Cost Baseline
b) Scope Statement
c) Schedule Baseline
d) Project Schedule

**Question 28:** During risk planning, you decided to make a contingency plan for delay in a critical task that can cause a chain reaction of task delays. To execute the plan, you decided to use "missing" some milestones as triggers. Where can you find a list of the project milestones?

a) Scope Baseline
b) WBS
c) Task Register
d) Schedule Plan

**Question 29:** You are the project manager of a "Do-it-Yourself" project for converting your garage into a small home gym. You recruited some of your friends to help you. You need to install a wooden floor for the gym. However, you discovered that the garage ground is not leveled which will make flooring installation difficult. After discussions with your friends, you decided to transfer the risk of poor installation conditions. What was the decision?

a) You will not install wooden floor
b) You will try to level the flooring with cement
c) You will install the wood anyway
d) You will hire a carpenter to install the wooden floor for you

Practice Questions

**Question 30:** The project manager was discussing which contract type is to be used for the project with the risk manager. The project scope involves constructing a high school building. The risk manager advised him/her to use a fixed cost contract. What might be the reason?

a) Contractors prefer this type of contract
b) This is the right type of contract for building schools
c) This type of contract will balance risks between the company and its contractors
d) The prices of building materials have been rising a great deal recently

**Question 31:** XYZ Steel Factory has been in business since 1977. The factory had a very successful history in the last decade and was the first to adopt many technologies like the use of an automated workflow HR system in 2004. There were some changes in senior management and an emphasis was made on risk management. A lot of money was spent on training and on preparing a risk manual. As the risk manager of a project to add a new steel furnace, where should you go to find the official risk matrix for XYZ Steel Factory?

a) Project Scope Statement
b) Project Scope Baseline
c) Organizational Environmental Factors
d) Organizational Process Assets

**Question 32:** Which one of the following motivation theories suggests that workers can be divided into those who like to take responsibility and those who don't?

a) McGregor Theory of X&Y
b) Maslow's Hierarchy of Needs
c) Herzberg's Theory
d) Two-factor Theory

# Chapter 8

**Question 33:** The project team gives priority to their day-to-day work, not to the project work. In which organizational structure does this take place?

a) Matrix
b) Projectized
c) Functional
d) Strong Functional

**Question 34:** You are managing a project to design a training system for all your company workers based on individual competencies. You work in the training department as the head of training section, and the company is functional in structure. You would like to use the expertise of a data analyst from the Statistics Department. What should you do?

a) Contact the Data Analyst directly and ask for her help
b) Contact the Manager of the Statistics Department and ask for the help of the Data
   Analyst
c) Contact the Manager of the Statistics Department through the Training Manager and   ask for the help of the Data Analyst
d) Contact the Data Analyst through the Training Manager and ask for the help of the
   Data Analyst

**Question 35:** You calculated the expected monetary value to be $245,000 in a $400,000 investment. What is the probability of this happening?

a) 61%
b) 0.61%
c) 1.6%
d) 16%

# Practice Questions

**Question 36:** How many communication channels are available for 6 people?

a) 12
b) 13
c) 14
d) 15

**Question 37:** You can choose between two projects to develop different children's toys. Find which toy should be developed based on the information provided in the figure below:

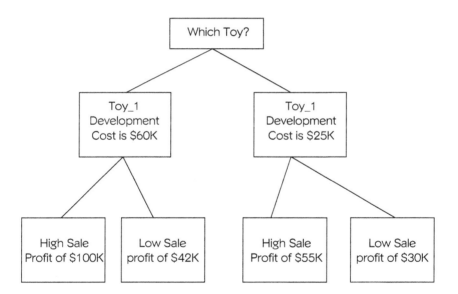

a) Toy 1
b) Toy 2
c) Both toys will yield the same profit
d) Both toys will lead to losses

Chapter 8

**Question 38:** Expert judgment can sometimes be effected by:

a) Poor Memory
b) Bias
c) Obsolete Technology
d) Misunderstanding

**Question 39:** You have just finished quantitative risk analysis and will start qualitative analysis tomorrow. What will be the most beneficial tool to use from the list below?

a) Risk Simulation Software
b) Performance Reports
c) Stakeholders Register
d) Change Log

**Question 40:** The chart that illustrates project tasks as a hierarchical representation is called:

a) Hierarchical Breakdown Structure
b) Risk Breakdown Structure
c) Tasks Breakdown Structure
d) Work Breakdown Structure

## Practice Questions

**Question 41:** During a risk identification meeting, the risk manager said that as much as 80% of all risks may be caused by only 20% of all possible causes. The risk manager was referring to:

a) Unequal Percentage Distribution
b) Inversely Proportioned Law
c) Pareto Law
d) The Law of the Tornado Diagram

**Question 42:** During risk identification, the risk manager suggested including high winds as a risk that may affect the construction project during the task of erecting scaffolding. However, the project manager said that high winds would never blow at that time of the year, so it shouldn't be considered. What did the project manager just do?

a) She anticipated
b) She assumed
c) She predicted
d) She was impolite to the risk manager

**Question 43:** You are managing a small project to add a biometric attendance control system to your company. You undertook risk management and made a complete risk register. However, you noticed that the SPI is 0.7. What should you do?

a) Do risk reassessment
b) Add more resources
c) Contact the supplier and tell him to speed up the delivery of materials
d) Implement your contingency plans

# Chapter 8

**Question 44:** ------------- is used to represent sensitivity analysis.

a) Tidal Diagram
b) Histogram
c) Tornado Diagram
d) Cause and Effect Diagram

**Question 45:** Which one of the following is a characteristic of the management reserve?

a) It is used for passively accepted risks
b) It is used for actively accepted risks
c) It is included in the project cost baseline
d) It is not included in the project cost baseline

**Question 46:** The Monte Carlo simulation is used for:

a) Finding which risks the project is more sensitive to
b) Establishing the probable effect(s) of risks on the whole project
c) Finding the expected monetary value for different options
d) Used to find thresholds for the risk matrix

**Question 47:** You want to use simulation in your project. To establish which distribution to use, you try to collect information (data) about the project tasks. The best information you are able to get is from employees who were involved in similar projects. You were able to get a most likely, least likely and an expected duration for most of the project tasks. Which distribution should you use?

a) Triangular Distribution
b) Normal Distribution
c) Uniform Distribution
d) Long Normal Distribution

**Question 48:** The technique that is used to find the probable cost/profit from different options is called?

a) Earned Value
b) Cost Tree Analysis
c) Decision Tree Analysis
d) Decision Matrix

**Question 49:** A risk manager was just assigned to a new project. He is very busy collecting information about the scope of the project and how complex it is. He is trying to find out how the project serves the overall company objectives. In addition, he is interviewing senior management and stakeholders to know how they perceive the importance of the project.
The risk manager is trying to establish:

a) Risk Plan
b) Risk Tolerance
c) Risk Acceptance Level
d) Risk Flexibility Rate

# Chapter 8

**Question 50:** In a communication model, the message is transferred from the sender to the receiver through a:

a) Medium
b) Dimension
c) Communication Method
d) Communication Technology

**Question 51:** You work in a major electronics company in Europe. You have been selected to run a project to manufacture a new mobile phone in China. The duration of the project is 8 months and you will be required to live in China for that period. The project team is made fully of Chinese staff. One day after a long meeting, you went to your office tired out, put your legs up on the desk and called the project secretary to tell her to make amendments to the communication plan. In the next few days, you noticed many mistakes in the plan and you started to wonder if the secretary paid any attention to your instructions. Why did this happen?

a) Due to the lack of competency on the part of the secretary
b) Inappropriate body language from the project manager that blocked communication
c) Not enough time given for the secretary to finish the plan
d) The project manager should send an official email to the secretary explaining the amendments

Practice Questions

**Question 52:** You just joined "Five Stars Toy Company" and were assigned a project to build a toy car for children. In one meeting, you heard the following conversation between two influential stakeholders:

Stakholder1: The color of the car should be red to resemble sports cars.
Stakholder2: I totally disagree, research shows that cars in silver sell more.

What should you do as a project manager?

a) Log this conflict in the issue log and negotiate a solution between the two parties
b) Log the conflict in the issue log and tell the stakeholders that the color will be   decidedby top management
c) Log this conflict in the conflict log and negotiate a solution between the two parties
d) Log the conflict in the conflict log and tell the stakeholders that the color will be decided by top management

**Question 53.** You are the risk manager of a project to manufacture new kitchen appliance for company XYZ. The company has been facing many financial troubles due to the last financial crisis and is hoping that the new product will improve its market presence. The project manager instructed you to prepare a presentation on the identified risks and their importance. The presentation has been scheduled for senior management. One hour before the meeting, you received a call from the project manager who informed you that the time allocated for your presentation was reduced to only 5 minutes and told you to bring only a one-slide presentation. Which of the following illustrations should you use?

a) Tornado Diagram
b) Scatter Diagram
c) Brainstorming Output
d) Network Diagram

**Question 54:** Which knowledge area is responsible for reviewing and approving change requests?

a) Project Integration Management
b) Project Communication Management
c) Project Risk Management
d) Project Procurement Management

**Question 55:** You are the DIY (do-it-yourself) project manager for converting your old Toyota MR-2 into an electric car. Your team members include friends and neighbors who have some mechanical experience. You made a WBS with the main tasks: remove engine, remove petrol tank, install electric motor, install batteries, check connection and test drive. To estimate how long the tasks will take, you searched for specialized forums on the Internet and asked several mechanics who undertook the same conversion before. However, your collected data is different. After careful review, you were able to assign the following durations for each task as most likely, least likely and expected. What estimation method can you use to compute durations with a fair amount of accuracy?

a) Earned Value Analysis
b) Three-point Estimation
c) Cause and Effect Analysis
d) Data Trends Estimation

**Question 56:** You are the sponsor of a road construction project in a rural area in Brazil. Your company is located in Egypt and you selected a certain project manager to lead this project. What might be the reasons?

a) She is good in developing WBS
b) She is good in working with Risk Simulation
c) She is good in working with multicultural teams
d) She is good in working on Earned Value Management

**Question 57:** The communication plan is used to:

a) List names of the stakeholders
b) Identify which information is to be sent and to whom
c) Call for meetings
d) Track and document changes in the contact information of the project team and stakeholders

**Question 58:** You can use ……………………… to rank the project stakeholders

a) Stakeholders Qualitative Analysis
b) Stakeholders Salience
c) Stakeholders Quantitative Analysis
d) Stakeholders Variance

**Question 59:** In the middle of a public park project, the project manager received a claim from the contractor asking for compensation due to an increase in the cost of the type of wood used for fencing. The project manager used a time and materials contract type and thought that the price of that type of wood was fixed. The project manager delegated you, as you are the risk manager, to look into the problem and reply to the contractor. After reviewing the contract, you verified that the wood used for fencing was identified as probable to undergo price increase, and therefore, the price was fixed in the contract. How will you inform the contractor?

a) As this might be a mistake on the contractor's part, you will give him a call
b) You will invite the contractor to a meeting to go over the contract
c) You will send an official letter from the project manager to the contractor supported by references to relevant sections of the contract
d) To avoid conflicts, you decided to ignore the matter and deal with it at the end of the project

Chapter 8

**Question 60:** SWOT analysis stands for:

a) Strengths, Weakness, Opportunities and Time
b) Strategies, Weakness, Opportunities and Threats
c) Strengths, Weakness, Opportunities and Threats
d) Strategy, Weakness, Opportunities and Time

**Question 61:** Which tool is used to check the reliability and accuracy of risk data?

a) Risk Data Quality Assessment
b) The RBS
c) Expert Judgment
d) Risk Matrix

**Question 62:** Good project performance usually means good risk management. To check your performance, which of the following tools can you use?

a) The Risk Register
b) Performance Indexes
c) Pareto Analysis
d) Tornado Diagram

## Practice Questions

**Question 63:** Which of the following is an example of risk avoidance?

a) Hiring a contractor to do a task you are not an expert in
b) Adding 'extra' days to the time baseline in case a task is delayed
c) Adding a management reserve
d) Canceling the project

**Question 64:** A person who always tries to avoid risks is sometimes called:

a) Risk Seeker
b) Risk Averse
c) Risk Avoider
d) Risk Taker

**Question 65:** After finishing the first major milestone, the project manager sent an updated risk register to all stakeholders via email. He sent an electronic file using MS Office 2007©. However, not all stakeholders had the software installed on their computers, and as a result, they couldn't view the file. This problem happened due to the wrong selection of:

a) Communication methods
b) Communication transition
c) Communication technology
d) Communication channels

# Chapter 8

# Answers

**1. Answer is a.** This is a straightforward question, but with many irrelevant information about the project. This is usually the case in many of the questions, especially scenario-based ones.

**2. Answer is b.** The trick in answering this question is that you should know that after risk control (i.e. when the project closes), most of the outputs will involve the updating of existing documents. The only answer from the given list that implies an update is answer 'b'. You can reason that during the risk management activities, you identified an improvement in the risk register template (like including a new column for risks owners' mobile numbers) and, as such, you should update the template for future projects.

Another way to answer the question is by eliminating wrong answers as shown in the table below:

| Answer | Why is it wrong? |
| --- | --- |
| a) Control Charts | This is a quality control tool |
| c) Risk Owners List | The list is developed in risk response, and in no logical way will it change at project end |
| d) Company Risk Probability and Impact definitions | The definitions are put at the risk planning stage. |

**3. Answer is c.** Interactive communication has advantages over pull and push in that it allows for clarification and discussions.

**4. Answer is b.** During the risk identification stage, you might identify "initial" responses along with risks. This can happen automatically especially for experienced people. However, the full and "official" risk response has to be documented in the risk register after the completion of the risk response planning.

**5. Answer is b.** You find the mean by adding the numbers and dividing by their count.

Mean = (2.3 + 4 + 6.5 + 6 + 7 ) / 5
= 25.8 / 5
= 5.16, which can be rounded off to 5.2

Note how close the numbers are.

**6. Answer is b.**

**7. Answer is d.** Remember that you will identify risk owners only after you design the risk response.

**8. Answer is b.** Prepare yourself for many similar questions. They depend on both memory and your ability to use reasoning and logic to find hidden information. In this question, first, you need to know the name of the technique used. The key word that will lead you is "consensus" which is a goal of the Delphi technique. Now, use your memory (or better yet, the chart I advised you to make at the beginning of the exam) to find where the technique is located.

**9. The question can be worded like this:**

You are the risk manager of the largest solar energy plant construction project in Arizona State. Your project will subcontract the manufacture of many components and will cover four countries: Italy, Japan, Mexico and the USA. The official language of the project is English. What is the best means of communication to be used in this project?

**Answer is d.** As English is not the official language in many of the listed countries, informal communication should be avoided. Informal language like the use of slang can foster different interpretations and result in misunderstandings

**10. Answer is b.** From the communication chapter, you know that there are different dimensions of communication. For the given situation, you will be communicating important information about the project progress, so the delivery should be done formally (i.e. either through reports or presentations). Presentations are preferred over reports because they allow for interactivity/discussion.

**11. Answer is a.** In answering the exam questions, you should always analyze the given problem and identify the basic cause. Missing a meeting can happen due to many reasons (how about being stuck in traffic?). The FIRST thing the project manager should do is to review the communication plan (before jumping to conclusions). He/she must first exclude the possibility that those stakeholders did not receive an invitation and were indeed included in the plan. After that, a series of actions can be taken, like asking them to state the reason for not coming.

Another possible question with the same answer can be: During a meeting, you noticed that not all stakeholders received the last update of the risk register. What is the first thing you need to do?

**12. Answer is a.** Remember that you can decrease the magnitude of risk by either reducing its probability or severity. By mitigating a risk, you don't prevent it from happening but you reduce its negative effect.

**13. Answer is b.** You should pay particular attention to your body language, especially when dealing with people from other cultures, as what might be acceptable in your culture might be considered offensive in other cultures. Your tone of voice is also important and can either facilitate your message or block it.

**14. Answer is c.** There are actually two risk tolerances: one for the organization and one for the specific project. The organization risk tolerance can be found from the organizational process assets. This tolerance will be modified for the specific project and will be included in the risk management plan.

**15. Answer is d.** Procedures are found in the process assets. What is the difference between a process and a procedure?

## 16. Answer

An example question can be as follows: A major project to construct a subway system in a city is underway. You were hired as a full time risk manager. You are currently investigating how much of the contingency reserve has been used. In what process is the risk manager at?

**Answer is 'd'**

The reason behind the answer can be: If the risk manager is investigating the amount of reserve that has been used up, he should be doing reserve analysis which is part of the risk monitoring process.

**17. Answer is b.** The idea in this question is that after you start project execution, you should not make changes without change requests and approvals.

| Answer | Description |
| --- | --- |
| a) Contact the local hiring agency to recruit a programmer ASAP | You can do that, but after approval. |
| b) Issue a change request (corrective action) to hire a new programmer) | Correct answer. |
| c) Issue a change request (preventive action) to hire a new programmer | The risk of possible delay due to insufficient number of programmers already happened, so you cannot prevent it by issuing a preventive action. |
| d) As the project is in the execution phase, there is nothing that can be done | Projects are dynamic. You can make changes, but they need to be controlled. |

**18. Answer is a.** You should not ignore stakeholders' requirements as the stakeholders- depending on their strength and interest - can delay the project or even "force" their requirements upon the project.

**19. Answer is a.** Since you are choosing between alternatives, you should use the decision tree technique. First, draw the decision tree and include the given costs and probabilities.

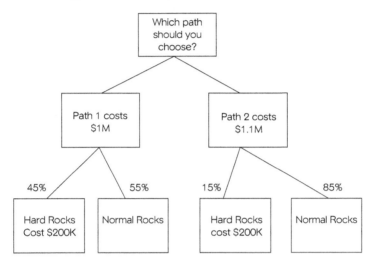

Cost of Path 1 = $1M + (0.45 * 200,000) = $1,090,000
Cost of Path 2 = $1.1M + (0.15 * 200,000) = $1,130,000

So, we should select Path1 because it will cost less. This question illustrates the importance of verifying our data (i.e. the quality of data used in calculation). For example, if the estimation of the probability was wrong, it could affect our calculations and lead us into making the wrong decision.

Another version of this question may give you a situation where you encounter 3 types of rocks: normal, medium and hard, and thus you must find the monetary value of all three types of rocks.

Remember, probability is always a hundred percent, so if you have two options and were given the probability of only one of the them, you can subtract it from 100 to find the other probability.

**20. Answer is b.** By having more safety engineers, you are decreasing the probability of injury, as it is their job to enforcw safety regulations. However, safety engineers cannot prevent accidents or absorb the negative results (i.e. like project delay).

**21. Answer is b.** The reason is that contingency plans are activated when triggers occur. The question mentions fast tracking, which is a technique used to compress the schedule by making sequential activities parallel to each other. Another technique to compress the schedule is called "crashing" which involves adding more resources to reduce the duration of a task.

**22. Answer is c.** Since the team is made of fresh graduates, they are more likely to be in need of direction. You can argue that this style has many disadvantages, but among the given answers, this one is the best. In the given situation, being autocratic has a better chance of helping the team to accomplish the project objectives.

**23. Answer is d.** From the question, we can guess that the project manager focuses on people more than tasks.

**24. Answer is b.** The main goal of quantitative risk analysis is to provide data on the probability of meeting project objectives (mainly time and money).

Practice Questions

**25. Answer is d.** Although not discussed in the book, the project charter is a very important document. It gives the official "go ahead" to the project. It contains high level information about the project (e.g. description, budget and milestones) and it officially identifies the project manager and specifies his/her level of authority. Project charters are signed by senior management, usually the CEO or the GM.

**26. Answer is a.** To answer this question and many others, you should be comfortable with the definitions of risk response strategies.

**27. Answer is b.** Assumptions are found in the scope statement.

**28. Answer is d.**

**29. Answer is d.** See the table below:

| Answer | Description |
| --- | --- |
| a) You will not install a wooden floor. | This is risk avoidance. |
| b) You will try to level the flooring with cement. | This is risk mitigation. |
| c) You will install the wooden floor anyway. | This is risk acceptance. |
| d) You will hire a carpenter to install the wooden floor for you. | This is risk transfer. |

**30. Answer is d.** The purpose of the fixed cost contract is to protect the project owner from unexpected variation(s) in cost (like the increase in the cost of materials).

**31. Answer is d.** Risk templates and definitions are found in the process assets. This is a typical exam question: It is supposed to be simple and straightforward, but surrounded with irrelevant information.

**32. Answer is a.** To answer this question, you need to know what the different theories suggest.

**33. Answer is c.**

**34. Answer is c.** This is a common situation in projects done inside functional structures. A functional structure gives ultimate authority over staff and resources to functional managers. For this reason, all requests should go through functional managers, especially those involving requesting services of staff. Notice how the answers are very close in wording which can be confusing especially in an exam which is being answered under time pressure.

**35. Answer is a.** Recall that

EVM = probability * investment.

So, probability is EVM divided by the investment amount. Note that all the wrong answers are purposely made to trick you if you miscalculate (e.g. if you divide the investment over the EVM).

**Possible Mistakes:** You might confuse the EVM with the investment amount due to sentence wording. Also, be careful about the % sign and know how to represent your answer, i.e. 0.6 is 60%, but 0.06 is 6% and 0.006 is 0.6%.

**36. Answer is d.** The formula for the communication channels is n(n-1)/2 = 6(6-1)2 = 30/2 = 15 channels.

**37. Answer is b.** You need to find the difference between the investment and the forecasted sale figures. Note that not all probabilities are given, but you can easily find them by subtracting the given probability from 100%.

For Toy 1, the expected monetary value

= investment − (profit from high sale + profit from low sales)
= 60,000 − (0.50 * 100,000 + 0.5 * 42,000) = $11,000

Similarly for Toy 2

= 25,000 − (0.4 * 55,000 + 0.6 * 30,000) = $15,000

So, we choose to develop Toy 2 as it is expected to yield more profit.

**38. Answer is b.** Remember that bias means to favor an outcome over another without being objective.

**39. Answer is a.** During quantitative risk analysis, you want to know the probability of your project getting completed as planned. To do that, you should use simulation software. As for the performance reports, you will use them in the last process of risk management. The stakeholders register is used for risk identification and the change log is given in the question to trick you.

**40. Answer is d.** WBS is frequently defined as a hierarchical representation of project tasks. Another potential question about the WBS is to ask you about work packages. Work packages are the simplest tasks in the WBS to which you can assign time and resources.

**41. Answer is c.** Note that the Pareto law is also called the 80/20 rule.

**42. Answer is b.** When we assume, we are basically confident something will happen without having a proof for that. In this question, the project manager takes it for granted that the high winds, which is anticipated to be a risk, will never happen. However, this assumption can be supported with historical information.

**43. Answer is a.** First, let us understand the question. The SPI is used to indicate how well your project is progressing. An SPI that is less than 1 indicates that the project is behind schedule, which is the case in the question. Now we can re-write the question as: The project is behind schedule, what should you do? Well, since you are in the risk monitoring and control stage, look for tools that can be used in that process. From the given answer choices, you should select 'risk reassessment', as it is most likely that the project is delayed due to new risks or existing ones that are having a greater impact on the project than was previously thought. Reassessment will allow you to redesign risk control, as needed. As for the other given answers, there is no information in the question telling you the reason for the delay, so it is better to choose the general answer. However, if the question states that the reason for the delay is the lack of resources, then you can select answer 'b'.

**44. Answer is c.**

**45. Answer is d.** All other answers are for the contingency reserve. Can you remember other characteristics of the management reserve?

**46. Answer is b.** See the table below:

| Answer | Why is it wrong? |
|---|---|
| a) Finding which risks the project is more sensitive to | This should be done through sensitivity analysis. |
| b) Establishing the probable effect of risks on the whole project | This is the correct answer. Monte Carlo is used for simulation which numerically tells you the chance of meeting the project objectives. |
| c) Finding the expected monetary value for different options | This is achieved by using decision tree analysis. |
| d) Used to find thresholds for the risk matrix | You use risk tolerance to identify thresholds. Also, you can use historical information or industry standards. |

**47. Answer is a.** To make a triangular distribution, you need three figures: a most likely, least likely and expected.

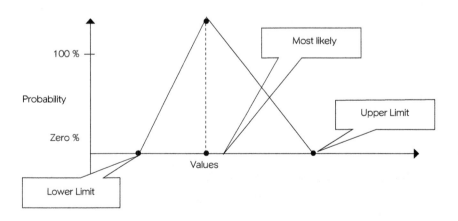

**48. Answer is c.** The key to know the answer is the use of "different options" in the question. Note how similar answers 'b' and 'c' are in wording.

**49. Answer is b.** All the activities that the risk manager is doing will help to identify risk tolerance. Remember that tolerance can be different for different projects and as such, the risk management plan contains only the tolerance level for its specific project.

**50. Answer is a.** you really need to know the components of the communication model to be able to answer this question correctly. Other questions on the same subject can be about the meaning of message decoding and the importance of feedback.

**51. Answer is b.** The information given in the question is not complete. We might never know the real reason for the mistakes in the secretary's assignment. However, we should look for relevant information and then make an intellectual guess. First, note that this project involves people from different cultures. Before the project manager met with the secretary, he had come from a long meeting and was tired, so we can guess that he was not in his best mood, which might have affected his tone of voice. In addition, the posture of the project manager, i.e. putting his legs on the table might have blocked the message from getting to the secretary. Let's try a new way of solving the question. Draw a sequence of pictures of the scenario and what possibly was going on the minds of the project manager and the secretary.

# Practice Questions

**52. Answer is a.** The scenario of this question describes an issue. PMBOK explains that issues arise when there is disagreement on some point and makes it the project manager's responsibility to resolve issues between stakeholders.

The best way to resolve issues is by negotiating a solution that is acceptable to all parties. However, first, the conflict has to be analyzed and understood completely. One of the best ways to achieve good negotiation is for each party to get in the other person's "shoes", which should foster a win-win solution.

Note how the given answers try to trick you into choosing between an issue log and a conflict log. You need to read this book to be able to choose between them (I did not mention a conflict log at all in this book). Another attempt to trick you is the statement saying that senior management will make the decision. You can reason that if the decision is to be made by senior management, then the conflict will not arise in the first place.

You can make many sub-questions based on this scenario as per the following table:

| No. | Possible Question | Possible Answers |
|---|---|---|
| 1 | What interpersonal skills are to be used in resolving this conflict? | Active Listening |
| 2 | What management skills are needed to resolve this conflict? | Negotiating |
| 3 | What is the first thing that has to be done? | Situational analysis |
| 4 | After the conflict is resolved, what must you do? | Update the project plan if the issue is resolved during project planning, and issue a change request if the issue is resolved during project execution. |
| 5 | How do you determine which stakeholder has more power? | By using the power/interest matrix |
| 6 | What tool in risk management can help you to find the cause of the conflict? | Root Cause Analysis |
| 7 | Where can you find the issue log? | In Project Documentation |
| 8 | What activities could the project manager have done in the past that would have made his job of resolving issues easier? | Building Trust |

53. Answer is a.

| Answer | Description |
|---|---|
| a) Tornado Diagram | It can be presented on one slide and will include the risks and their impact(s) |
| b) Scatter Diagram | This will not contain information on risks |
| c) Brainstorming Output | It will contain a list of risks, but it will not be organized and usually takes time to explain |
| d) Network Diagram | This will not contain information on risks |

**54. Answer is a.** Change requests are processed through the processes available in project integration management.

**55. Answer is b.** Remember that you use three-point estimation when you know the data points as given in the question.

**56. Answer is c.** Not enough information has been given and, thus, you should select the BEST logical answer. All of the given answers have important qualities, but for a project to be done in another country, knowing how to work with people of other cultures should be the number one quality. All other qualities can be delegated, but not the selected answer.

## Practice Questions

**57. Answer is b.**

**58. Answer is b.** You can also use a power/interest grid. Another way to ask the question would be: Which tools can be used to rank stakeholders based on their power, legitimacy and urgency?

**59. Answer is c.** This is a classical question. You can have hundreds of scenarios but it boils down to that: important information (especially with external parties and where money is involved) must be sent officially and in writing.

**60. Answer is c.** Answering this question not only requires knowledge of the subject, but also concentration to avoid being tricked by similar words or terms.

**61. Answer is a.** The risk data quality assessment ensures that the data on risk is accurate and effective for risk management.

**62. Answer is b.** Performance indexes include the schedule performance index (SPI) and the cost performance index (CPI). They are part of earned value management and will show how a project is actually performing.

**63. Answer is d.** This is an example of the most extreme case of risk avoidance. By canceling the project, the risk will NEVER happen (however, you will never harness the benefits of the project which may be substantial).

**64. Answer is b.** And the one who likes to take risks is called a risk seeker.

**65. Answer is c.** This question tests your understanding of communication terminology.

# Chapter 9:
## Can you do it?

Chapter 9

# Can you do it?

Don't worry, just a little more. At this point you covered everything you need to know from the PMBOK. However, this is a professional certificate and it is from the PMI, so there must be more. The PMI wants this certificate to capture what real risk managers do. So, they (the PMI) made a survey to know how risk management is practiced. This survey was called RDS (Risk Delineation study). Of course this is just a background so don't start taking notes. Ok, so based on the result of the survey, the PMI issued (or updated) an exam outline document of 20 pages which describes what skills are needed for the exam. But hold your horses, don't jump and download this document. You can, its free, but it will not help you much. For example, you will find things in it like:
Candidates must have knowledge of communication skills.
But this is already covered in the book. However, reading the document I found few terms not discussed in the PMBOK like "risk appetite". I will discuss these concepts here.

The following are the reason why I didn't include these concepts in the previous chapters. These reasons have a main theme of: " you don't need to worry that much":

1  Because they are not part of the PMBOK and I believe the exam will focus more on terms and terminology used from there
2  Because by now, after reading through this book, you are in a very good standing in terms of understanding risk management. Thus it should take you much less effort to understand new concepts in risk management.
3  In the most part, these terms are not really new, just another representation of things you already know. Take for example the term: Risk Taxonomy. If you know that taxonomy is a field of biological science where animals are classified then it will be easy for you to guess that Risk Taxonomy is some sort of risk classification. Such knowledge might help you answer / guess few questions.

This chapter is divided into two parts: in the first I will discuss the new terms. The second will act as a general recap of what you learned so far.

## Part-1: Additional Risk Concepts

**-Risk Appetite:** you know what is an appetite. Now add the word risk to it, what you will get? Simply it means how much risk you are willing to eat (take). This of course will differ from a stakeholder to another and from a project to another.

> *Note:* as a reminder there are types of stakeholders attitude to risks. Not every one approaches them in the same way. There are the risk averse, tolerant and seeker. Usually projects in the government sectors are more averse toward risks and entrepreneurial projects (new business adventures) are risk seekers.

**-Heuristics:** this is a physiological term referring to A way of taking decisions. When you can't research a problem for some reason, you use your experience to find a quick solution. Example is "rules of thumbs" and "educated guesses" which are fast but may not be the best solutions. Link to risk management is clear. Such fast decisions can have risks of including many assumptions and errors.

**-Force Field Analysis** is a decision-making technique. The reason for so many tools for decision-making is that a good project manager should be able to explain the reason of a decision (i.e. he/she have a logic behind it, an "impulse" or "feeling" doesn't qualify here). So lets go back to force field analysis. For any decisions there will be positives and negatives. Your aim is to add them and see if the result will be positive or negative. To do that you need to give a score for each force. So for example, if I want to buy a used BMW the analysis can look like this

So my decisions will be not to buy it because the negatives outweigh the positives.

**-Bowtie analysis:** is a way to "tie" between the cau ses and results of an event (risk happening). You put the event in the middle and causes and effects on either side. It will look like a tie

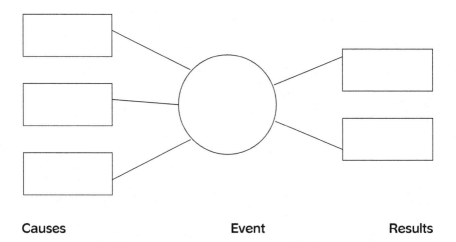

Causes　　　　　　　　　Event　　　　　　　　　Results

This is a good way of thinking about risks because you can draw it. It can also serve as a communication tool.

### -ISO31000

ISO stands for "International Standards Organization". It issues famous standards like the ISO-9001. The 31000 is on risk management. The most important part of this ISO for the RMP, is the idea of "continues improvement". ISO standards in general focus allot on this idea. Everything can be improved upon, where mistakes are identified and resolved.

In the exam you might be asked on how to improve the risk

management process in your organization. The answer can be: using lessons learnt, reviewing templates or analyzing the effectiveness of your risk identification. Again, no need to get into detail, just know that an international standard on risk management exists and that you can (and should) improve on your risk management processes. .

As you can imagine, most of this document ( isu 31000 ) is very similar to the risk chapter in the PMBOK. After all, risk management is a mere risk identification, assessment and control. Not much can be changed. However, you need to have an open mind that people can use whatever terms they want to describe something. For example, in the ISO31000 there is some thing called risk "treatment". I believe you will not find a trouble figuring out that this refers to risk "control".

-**Affinity diagram** is very simple and straightforward way of organizing and grouping ideas. You simply record different ideas on yellow stickers, then try to think of the best way to group them. Using yellow stickers is not mandatory of course but it will make it easy to stick one in a place then move it. You will use a wall to put the stickers on for better display. The diagram will look like columns of yellow stickers where each column representing a general area.

-**Nominal group** is a way of reaching people agreement on some ideas. Like brainstorming, participant are encouraged to put their ideas. Then everyone will vote on the ideas. The result will be a list of prioritized ideas where the best idea will be the one with the highest votes.

- **Risk attribute** characteristics of risks like category, type, probability, and impact.

-**Risk prompt list** is a checklist but with a category of risk (i.e. It will not list specific risks). For example, you will not find an item of "staff resigns", but a more general category of "People Risks". The idea of these lists is to push (prompt) you to think and brainstorm of risks under the category.

-**Fault Tree Analysis FTA** is a way to find the basic causes of an event ( risk). It follows the same idea of WBS. You put the risk on the top of the page and then think of events that can lead to it.

-**Visualization** is a term used when data are represented by graphs or sketches. Visualization make understanding easier. For example, a risk matrix a way of visualizing risks importance in relation to each other.

You can also use a 3d risk matrix. So, for the exam, just know that visualization is a good way to foster understanding of an issue.

- **Risk connectivity analysis** this is a new way of looking at risks. You know that risk is a factor of probability and severity. But what about risks being connected to other risks. The idea, is that a small risk can be connected to other risks which makes it more risky. what I mean by conectivity is if a risk is connected to another then if one happens the other will also happen. Usually a software is used to produce connectivity analysis. The software will create a network like diagram showing what risks are connected to others. This idea gives another prospective on how to view risks and help identify "hidden" risks that can cause big problems.

- **Analogous estimation:** here you estimate prices based on past experience. For example, if you changed 4 tires for your Toyota Camry at a cost of 500 $ few months ago, then you can estimate that it will cost about 500$ to change the tires for your wife's Honda accord. Same thing for projects, where costs for similar work tend to be similar. However, this is not an exact estimation and thus there will be risks in using it. This is called sometimes a " top down " estimation because you get the estimate as a whole and in one go.

- **Parametric estimation** here you estimate the price of service or product based on numbers you have. For example, if one meter of an electrical cable costs 10$, then a 5 meter cable will cost you 50 dollars. This is more accurate than analogous estimation.

- **Bottom up estimation** from its name you can guess that this is used to get the price of something by adding the costs of its components.

-**Scenario Planning** is a way to identify possible risks. From the current situation of your company/project you make a story (scenario) of what can happen in the future. For example, you can make a scenario that some conditions will change like fuel prices will go up or there will be shortage in skilled people in the job market. Based on these scenarios you discuss how your company or project can deal with this possible situation.

> **Note:** the oil company "Shell" used scenario planning to prepare for the oil crises in the 1970s. You can search the net on that case.

> **Note:** scenario planning is used to validate your risk response. For example, you might identify a risk in your project that an equipment will fail. You might decide to put a control of having money in the contingency reserve to rent a replacement. But will this really work? You need to make a scenario that the equipment failed and you go to rent the replacement equipment. Will it be available? Will it function as the equipment you already have?

- **Regression analysis and correlation** these are statistical concepts: egression is used to find weather two variables are connected. Meaning if one changes will it cause the other to change or not? Correlation, on the other hand, investigates the type of the relationship. A formula is used to find a "correlation coefficient" with value between -1 and +1. If the result is positive then the two variable move together. If the result is negative, then if one variable increase the other will decrease and vise versa. If the value is zero, then there is no relationship.

- **Cost benefit analysis** this is a study done before a company starts a project. The expected profit is calculated by subtracting the project cost from the expected return. If the project is expected to create more revenue than cost, then it should be done. A famous tool to calculate the expected profit is called return on investment or ROI. This tool involves financial calculations, which is outside the scope of this book.

Note that money is not the only thing that projects are made to achieve. For example, many governmental projects are made to improve living conditions for citizens where it is not applicable to use financial calculations. Other calculations can be used like the expected degree of satisfactions and improvements in conditions.

- **Trend analysis** is a good way to predict the future. From historical data you can guess the direction of the future. For example, in a construction project, is the sub contractor failed in "concrete" testing 5 times out of 7, you can guess the next time have a great chance of also failing.

## Part-2: Recap

This section is based on the RMP exam guidelines issued from the PMI to the training providers, so pay attention. Here I will discuss all the areas you need to be comfortable with for the exam. You will see a table with tasks you must be able to perform as a risk manger in real life. If you are still not comfortable with a task then you need to go back and study the theory behind it.

| Can You ? | Yes | No | If No |
|---|---|---|---|
| We talked about the threshold of risks. For example, in a project a stakolder can accept 5% increase in budget but no more. Can you determine this? . | ☐ | ☐ | Read more about risk tolerance. Understand that stakeholders are important. |
| Can you improve on the risk management process? For example, the tools you use for risk identification. You might find out that more risks really occurred in a project than initially identified. This should trigger a process improvement. You can, for example, suggest to change the method used for identification. | ☐ | ☐ | You need to accept that improvement is required. You can know that improvement is needed from lessons learnt and from risk audits. |
| Can you create a strategy for risk management for your project? By strategy I mean simply the risk plan, you know, things like how often risks meeting will be conducted, how much resources will be assigned and the matrix you will use. Remember that the type of matrix you use is a big element in determining your strategy. A more detailed matrix will yield better risk assessment but will also take more time to use. What will determine your strategy (i.e. risk plan), is the project objectives and of course the stakeholders tolerance to risk. | ☐ | ☐ | Read about the contents of the risk plan and about the project scope and stakeholders tolerance |

# Can you do it?

| | | | |
|---|---|---|---|
| Can you evaluate the effectiveness of your project risk management ? This can be done during the project execution | ☐ | ☐ | This can be done using the tools in the last risk process like audits and trend analysis. Remember, during the first process, i.e. the risk planning you should identify that you will use tools to check the effectiveness of your risk management. |
| Can you make others in your project team appreciate the value of risk management? What about the stakeholders? This is not an easy task because risk management talks about the future. Things might or might not happen. Risk management also require effort and budget | ☐ | ☐ | This depends on two things: your interpersonal skills and your own understanding of risk management. |
| Can you train your team and stakeholders on risk management activities | ☐ | ☐ | To train your team you need to have good grasp of risk managemnt |
| Can you identify your project stakeholders risk tolerance? Is it low or high? Do they have big appetite or small? Do they seek risks or want to avoid them? Also will this change during the project?<br><br>Can you also manage their expectation? | ☐ | ☐ | You can do that by interviews and meetings. Also by looking at historical data<br><br>As for expectation, to manage that you can use different techniques, but should start with a stakeholders matrix |

# Chapter 9

| | | | |
|---|---|---|---|
| Get consensus from stakeholders on how important are different risks? | ☐ | ☐ | By involving them in risk prioritization like qualitative assessment using a risk matrix. |
| Communicate risks to stakeholders? | ☐ | ☐ | You need to know about communication and stakeholders management |
| Foster commitment to risk control from the people in charge of a particular risk response (i.e. risk owners) | ☐ | ☐ | You can do this by involving the people whom you expect will own risks in the risks identification, assessment and response activities. Also their roles and responsibilities must be clear to them. Communication and involvement is key here |
| Share project performance information | ☐ | ☐ | You should include risk reports in your communication plan. Also invite concerned people to risk meetings. |
| Can you determine a risk level? | ☐ | ☐ | By the formula, risk = chance * impact |
| Improve risk identification | ☐ | ☐ | You can use different tools to identify risks. Also you need to review the documents that can contain risks like cost plan, schedule and scope |

# Can you do it?

| | | | |
|---|---|---|---|
| Assess risks using qualitative and quantitative tools | ☐ | ☐ | Read more about the tools risk matrix and simulation |
| Estimate how much your contingency reserve must be. | ☐ | ☐ | Read about risk response strategies and risk acceptance. |
| Reflect risks in your project budget and schedule | ☐ | ☐ | After doing your risk response and before project execution you need to "communicate" any changes affecting other plans. This is done using change request. |
| Validate your risk response plan to ensure project succeeds. | ☐ | ☐ | You are concerned here with " will my risk response actually work?". Scenario planning is suggested by PMI for such validation. You basically make a story that the risk actually happened and then investigate with an open mind if the control you put will work or not. |
| Document your risks and keep updated information | ☐ | ☐ | Use risk register and update it frequently |

| | | | |
|---|---|---|---|
| Integrate (coordinate) risk management with other project activities | ☐ | ☐ | Here your skill as project manager will show. You need to look at the big picture and link different components together. Change request is a useful tool to link changes between the originating document and affected document |
| Produce and communicate risks through reports | ☐ | ☐ | Risk register is the best report |
| Ensure risk is controlled during project execution and any residual risks are managed | ☐ | ☐ | Through continues risk reassessment. Remember that risk management doesn't stop through the life of the project. New risks emerge and will needs to be identified, assessed and controlled |
| Analyze risk performance against project metrics | ☐ | ☐ | Review the tool of technical performance measurement in project control process. For example, was a particular task completed in the time specified? |

| Update your risk plan | ☐ | ☐ | When new information becomes available you need to update the plan. For example, the risk plans contains roles and responsibilities. If a new member join the risk team, this should be reflected in the plan. |
|---|---|---|---|
| Capture lessons learned relating to risk management | ☐ | ☐ | You can get this easily by being alert and recording positives and negatives you encountered in the project |
| Use advanced techniques in risk management. Expect simple questions hear. Knowing the terms and reading the "essentials" chapter should do. | ☐ | ☐ | Like simulation and modeling. Also scenario planning and risk connectivity analysis. Such advance techniques require specialized soft wares. Statistics is also important here. |

Chapter 8

# After you Pass?

I wish you the best of luck in achieving your goal and getting the certificate. After you pass, I suggest that you do the following:

- Ask your manager to send congratulatory note to you via the company's public email
- Take a day off
- Print new business cards to reflect your new credential
- Dig deeper into risk management (especially risk simulation). There are other institutes and organizations that have excellent standards and guidelines on Project Risk Management, and they are worth checking out
- Play the rule of a "good deviant" and encourage project managers in your company to practice risk management. You can arrange with your training section head to offer training and coaching sessions for your co-workers
- Don't forget to drop me a line at alk.books@gmail.com with comments about your experience, this book and the exam

# References:

Project Management Institute A Guide to the Project Management Body of Knowledge (PMBOK® Guide) - 5th Edition, Project Management Institute, Inc., 2013.

RMP Exam Guidelines, electronic copy, PMI.com, Sept. 2013

www.dictionary.com

# INDEX

Accept 44, 65
Active Acceptance 78
Activity Cost Estimation 83
Activity Duration Estimation 83
Assumptions 2, 30
Asymmetrical Triangular Distribution 26
Autocratic Leadership 35
Average 14
Avoid 75, 76

Baselines 30,
Bell shaped distribution 28
Beta Distribution 27
Brainstorming 45, 51
Bureaucratic Leadership 36

# C

Change Requests 49, 58, 86
Charismatic Leadership 35
Checklist Analysis 68.99.102
Communication 44

# INDEX

Communication blockers 47
Communication Channels 39
Communication Management Plan 85
Communication Skills 50
Communication Technology 49
Conflict Resolution 50
Contingency Planning 80
Contingency reserve 140, 143
Contract Decisions 142
Contract Types 29
Control Charts 34
Corrective Actions 87
Cost Performance Index 158
Cost Reimbursable Contract 29

## D

Data Gathering 136
Decision Trees 17, 75
Democratic Leadership 170
Diagramming Techniques 68
Dimensions of Communication 190
Documentation Review 66, 99

## E

Earned Value Analysis (EV) 20
Enhance 75, 78

Enterprise Environmental Factors 84, 99
Expected Monetary Value (EMV) 16,
Expert Judgment 51, 65, 72
Exploit 75, 77, 138, 141

## F

Fallback Plans 95, 142, 147
Fixed Price Contract 29
Functional Structure 38

## G

Gantt chart 33

## H

Herzberg's Theory 38
Histogram 34

# I

Influence Diagram 69, 128
Interview 67, 72
Interviews and Expert Judgment 72
Ishikawa Diagram 69

# L

Laissez-faire Leadership 35
Leadership Styles 35
Lognormal Distribution 28

# M

Management reserve 78
Maslow's Hierarchy of Needs 37
Mathematics 134
Matrix 13
Matrix Organization 40
Mean 14
Mitigate 75, 77, 79
Modeling and Simulation 21
Monte Carlo 24

# N

Negotiation 50, 203
Network Diagram/PERT/CPM 31
Normal Distribution 28

# O

Opportunity 68, 71
Organizational Process Assets 85, 86
Organizational Structure 38

# P

Pareto Analysis/Law or the 34 Rule 34
Passive Acceptance 78.143
People Oriented Leadership 36
Performance Measurement 82
Performance Reports 85
Planning Meetings 64
Potential Responses 92
Power/Interest Grid 51
Preventive Actions 87
Probability Distribution 26
Process Flowcharts 69
Project Documentation 84
Project Management Plan 90
project phases 5
Projectized Structure 38

# INDEX

## Q

Quality of the Risk Data 71
Quality Management Plans 83
Quality Tools 33

## R

Reserve Analysis 82, 99
Residual Risks 95, 142, 144
Risk Audits 81, 96
Risk averse 185
Risk Categorization 71, 93
Risk Identification 5, 6, 7
Risk Management 2, 6, 13
risk management plan 88
risk matrix 13, 70
Risk Monitoring and Control 6, 58, 81, 95
Risk owners 90, 139, 143
Risk Planning 5, 6, 58
Risk Reassessment 81
Risk Register 45
Risk Response Planning 5, 58, 60
Risk tolerance 65, 79
Risk Urgency Assessment 72, 99, 104
RMP 2, 5, 6
Root Cause Identification 67

## S

Salience 52
Scatter Diagram 35
Schedule Performance Index 21
Scope Baseline 83, 99
Scope Statement 83, 158
Secondary Risks 95, 142
Sensitivity Analysis 28
Share 45, 52
Simulation 21, 23
Stakeholder Classification 51
Stakeholder Identification 51
Stakeholders 44
Stakeholders register 46
Standard Deviation 14
Status Meetings 81
SWOT Analysis 68

## T

Task oriented Leadership 36
The "Memorize then Understand" Framework 4
The Interactive Method 48
The Pull Method 48
The Push Method 48
The Risk Model 12
Threat 68
Three-point Estimation 73
Time and Materials Contract 183
Tornado Diagram 29

Transfer 75
Triangular Distribution 179
Triggers 194
Two-factor theory 38, 173

# U

Uniform Distribution 179

# V

Variance and Trend Analysis 82

# W

Watch List 93, 95
Work Breakdown Structure (WBS) 32
Workarounds 87, 143

# NOTES

# NOTES

# NOTES

# INSIDE BACK COVER

# BACK COVER

CPSIA information can be obtained
at www.ICGtesting.com
Printed in the USA
LVOW05s1752060717
540474LV00021B/338/P

9 781492 761174